Edition KWV

Die „Edition KWV“ beinhaltet hochwertige Werke aus dem Bereich der Wirtschaftswissenschaften. Alle Werke in der Reihe erschienen ursprünglich im Kölner Wissenschaftsverlag, dessen Programm Springer Gabler 2018 übernommen hat.

Weitere Bände in der Reihe http://www.springer.com/series/16033

Karin Möllering

Inventory Rationing

A New Modeling Approach Using Markov Chain Theory

Springer Gabler

Karin Möllering
Wiesbaden, Germany

Bis 2018 erschien der Titel im Kölner Wissenschaftsverlag, Köln
Dissertation der Wirtschaftswissenschaftlichen Fakultät der Westfälischen Wilhelms-Universität Münster, 2006

Edition KWV
ISBN 978-3-658-24254-1 ISBN 978-3-658-24255-8 (eBook)
https://doi.org/10.1007/978-3-658-24255-8

Library of Congress Control Number: 2019934951

Springer Gabler

This Springer Gabler imprint is published by the registered company Springer Fachmedien Wiesbaden GmbH part of Springer Nature
The registered company address is: Abraham-Lincoln-Str. 46, 65189 Wiesbaden, Germany

Zwei Dinge sind zu unserer Arbeit notwendig: Unermüdliche Ausdauer und die Bereitschaft, etwas, in das man viel Zeit und Arbeit gesteckt hat, wieder wegzuwerfen.
Albert Einstein

Friends of mine once said about their time reading for a PhD, "If I had known what it cost me, I would never have started" and characterized the four years as the honeymoon, in which everything is exciting and you are overconfidential, the paniking year in which you realize that you have not done a lot yet and are no longer sure wether you will be able to deliver, the third year during which you will work very hard and the rewarding year at the end. Now that I have finished my degree I know how much truth those words contained. And I would like to take the opportunity to thank all those who stood up to me throughout the last four years.

First of all, I would like to thank my supervisor, Prof. Ulrich Thonemann, for offering me the possibility to work on a fascinating topic. Discussions with him were fruitful and motivating. And he helped me especially with the second part of Einstein's remark on academic research.

Prof. Edward Anderson and Dr. Gal Raz kindly invited me for a research stay at the Australian Graduate School of Management, Sydney. They were very encouraging and always had a lot of time and an open ear for my questions and problems. Some of the results presented in this thesis originate here.

Also, I thank Prof. Ulrich Müller-Funk for agreeing to write the second opinion and valuable ideas for future work. Prof. Herbert Kuchen served as third examiner in my defense.

Thanks also go to my fellow Phd students and colleagues at the seminar in Münster and Cologne, for their support and friendship. Dr. Kai Hoberg, Alexander Weyers and Jeanette Seifert proof-read parts of this thesis. Felix

Papier additionally worked his way through the proofs. Our student aides, Analena, Claudia, Eva, Jan, Katja, and Kathrin, organized a lot of the literature and saw for timely extensions and returns. To all of you as well as Andreas, Christel, Hendrik, Karsten, Marc, Marcel, Silke and Ulf: It was a pleasure working with you (and more).

Finally, a lot of people enouraged me to start this PhD and they all put up with my moods and - especially during the last half year - with the reduced time I had for them. My family was a source of great support. And a special thanks goes to Tim who probably "suffered" most.

Cologne, January 2007 Karin Möllering

Contents

List of Tables

List of Figures

List of Abbreviations

ADI	advanced demand information
AP	aggregation policy
AV	averaging policy
c.d.f.	cumulative distribution function
cf.	confer
CPU	central processing unit
CRP	constant rationing policy
cts.	continuous
ed.	editor, edition
e.g.	exempli gratia
et al.	et alii
FCFS	first come, first served
GDP	gross domestic product
HP	Hewlett-Packard
i.i.d.	independent and identically distributed
i.e.	id est
LCL	linear critical level policy
NPO	next period optimization policy
p.d.f.	probability density function
per.	periodic
pp.	pages

resp.	respectively
r.v.	random variable
SP	separation policy
vs.	versus
WIP	work-in-process
w.r.t.	with respect to

List of Symbols

α, α_i	required α-service level (of class i)
$\overline{\alpha}$	demand-weighted average α-service level
β, β_i	required β-service level (of class i)
B_t, B_{it}	(total) backorders (of class i) in period t
B, B_i	(total) backorders (of class i) in steady state
B_i^{XY}	class i backorders in steady state under policy XY
CL, CL_k	critical level (on diagonal k)
CL_t^{XY}	critical level in period t under policy XY
CL^{XY}	expected critical level under policy XY
CL_i^S	minimal critical level satisfying the service constraint for class i given order-up-to level S
c_o, c_u	unit overage and underage cost per period
D_t, D_{it}	(total) demand (of class i) in period t
D, D_i	(total) demand (of class i) in steady state
d	period of a Markov chain
ETC, ETC^{XY}	expected total cost per period (under policy XY)
$EX, E[X]^+$	expectation of the (positive part of the) r.v. X
$f_{ij}^{(n)}$	probability to enter state j starting in state i for the first time after n steps
$F, F^{-1}, \overline{F}$	cumulative distribution function, its inverse, $1 - F$
h	unit holding cost per period

$\Im$	state space of a Markov chain
I_t, I	on-hand inventory after order arrival at the beginning of period t, of a period in steady state
IH_t, IH, IH^{XY}	on-hand inventory at the end of period t, of a period in steady state (under policy XY)
IO_t, IO	inventory on order at the beginning of period t, of a period in steady state
κ	constant of the linear critical level policy
λ_i	parameter of the Poisson distribution (demand of class i)
LT	lead time
m_{ii}	expected return time of state i
N	truncation value
ν	weight factor of the linear critical level policy
p, p_i	unit penalty cost per period (of class i)
$\overline{p}$	demand-weighted average period unit penalty cost
$P, P^{(n)}$	(n-step) transition matrix
$p_{ij}, p_{ij}^{(n)}$	(n-step) transition probability from state i to j
π_x, π_x^N	invariant probability of state x (with transition matrix truncated at N)
$(\pi_x)_{x\in\Im}, (\pi_x^N)_{x\in\Im}$	invariant distribution (with matrix truncated at N)
Q, Q_t	order quantity (in period t)
R	review period
s	reorder point
S, S^{XY}	order-up-to level (under policy XY)
S_i^0	Minimal order-up-to level to meet class i service constraint if $CL = 0$
T	index of the Markov chain, here $T = \mathbb{N}$
X_t	state of a Markov chain in period t, also: random variable

Z_k^{CL}	expected total cost with order-up-to level $S = k + CL$ and critical level CL
Ω	set of potentially optimal parameter constellations
$\leq_{st}, \geq_{st}$	stochastically smaller resp. larger

If necessary, we use superscripts $\cdot^{S,CL}$ to indicate dependencies on the decision variables S and CL. The superscript $\cdot^{*}$ indicates optimality. Specific realizations of random variables are denoted by small letters.

Chapter 1

Introduction

The success of Japanese companies in the second half of the 20th century has lead to an increased interest in inventory management. Typically, these companies operated with far less inventory than their Western counterparts. While initially the attention focused on the inventory within the production process, it has meanwhile also turned towards raw materials and finished goods. With 37.5% the latter presents the major part of the total inventory kept by US manufacturing companies (Survey of Current Business, April 2006). Lower inventory leads to less fixed capital and allows companies to react more flexible to market changes. Thus well-managed inventory might lead to a competitive advantage. Chen et al. (2005) provide empirical evidence that poor inventory management can harm a company's shareholder value.

The last decades have additionally seen an increasing diversity of customer expectations and growing competitive pressure for a wide variety of industries. To cope with those customer demands while maintaining a competitive offer, many companies have grouped their customers. This might be an internal process where customers are assigned a certain priority, e.g. based on annual sales volume, or a result of customers having signed up for special services. The segmented customer basis allows implementing an inventory management approach that resembles the yield management practised in the airline or hotel industries: Demand fulfillment for low priority customers

K. Möllering, *Inventory Rationing*, Edition KWV,
https://doi.org/10.1007/978-3-658-24255-8_1

might be refused or delayed in order to reserve stock for more important clients.

1.1 Motivation

Our research was originally motivated by an application at a European mobile communications provider. Some service parts are used at different levels of the telecommunication network, for instance in antennas and network computers. If a part fails in an antenna, the antenna goes down. If the same part fails in the network computer, the network computer goes down and about 30 antennas become unavailable. Thus the failure of this part in the network computer causes at least 30 times higher penalty cost than in the antenna.

In such situations, the approach outlined above helps to reduce costs because we reduce the number of expensive shortages. However, to apply this strategy two core questions have to be answered: Firstly, what is the optimal strategy? The formulation before suggests that one demand occurs after the other. In a lot of practical situations, this is not the case. Demands are not unit-sized and are collected over a certain time interval. In these situations, it is not immediately obvious in which way the available inventory should be divided amongst the different customer classes. For instance, demand from the highest customer class could always be filled if there is enough inventory or each customer class obtains a share that corresponds to its overall importance. Additionally, there is not only the delivery, but also the replenishment that has to be controlled. Secondly, the characterization of a strategy as such does not necessarily include a way to derive the optimal parameters. Thus optimization is the other question that requires an answer.

Intuitively, a lot of aspects of such a strategy are clear: For instance, it seems reasonable that the point after which we do not deliver anymore to low priority customers is lower if we expect a significant replenishment in the near future. Thus the orders in the pipeline have to be tracked. Unfortunately, this is exactly the point that most existing research tries to avoid. Only for unit-sized demands and assuming that both, demands of different classes and replenishments, cannot occur simultaneously, the optimal strategy has been completely characterized.

1.2 Research Objectives

Our main objective is to provide and optimize a mathematical model for more practical situations. Orders are not placed whenever a demand occurs but at certain discrete time instances. Demands are not necessarily unit-sized and demands of different priority (including waiting customers) may be observed at once. Furthermore, the time between placing an order and order arrival is greater than zero.

Building a mathematical model, it is tempting to include a maximum of real-life aspects. But the main contribution of a model lies in its solution. Thus simplifications and abstractions cannot be avoided completely. We restrict our attention to two customer classes and assume that a certain control policy is in place, the so-called *critical level policy*. Under this policy, if the inventory hits or drops below this rationing level, low priority customers are no longer served. In our context of larger incoming orders and demands, the order of events is decisive in which this policy is enforced. Cost-optimally, upon arrival of stock, all high priority customers should be considered before low priority customers, independent of the real sequence in which the demand occurred. This includes also all waiting customers. Although this is easy to see and to state verbally, this affects the mathematical tractability.

For constant critical levels, we present a new modeling approach based on a Markov chain with multi-dimensional states. This approach allows us to optimize the policy parameters in the presence of lead time and obeying by the cost-optimal sequence of events. We apply this approach to two problems. In one case, the two customer classes are prioritized based on the cost associated with each period that the customer has to wait. The second problem addresses the case in which the two customer classes require a different level of service.

As a second objective, we want to get some insight into the advantages of state-dependent critical levels as opposed to constant critical levels. We therefore introduce two state-dependent rules of setting the critical levels that allow us to maintain the advantage of a simple-to-implement strategy and evaluate the benefits.

1.3 Outline

To solve a mathematical model, the processes and characteristics that are supposed to be modeled have to be identified. Additionally, a certain amount of mathematics is required. In line with this observation, this thesis is divided into three parts: One part introducing the subject of inventory control, one part laying the mathematical foundations and finally the part introducing our model. Figure 1.1 gives an overview of this thesis.

The first part (Chapters 2 and 3) introduces stochastic inventory control. Chapter 2 focuses on general aspects of inventory management. While inventory control is concerned with the steering of stock in a specific environment, inventory management additionally includes all efforts influencing the environment e.g. by reducing lead times or quality defects (Zipkin 2000). We give evidence for the importance of inventory management, provide reasons for holding inventories, classify inventories into different types and look into the costs and service requirements associated with holding inventory. In Chapter 3, we concentrate on inventory control and identify decisive characteristics of the environment that have to be considered in the control of inventory. We provide an overview of the most common control policies and optimize a periodic review control policy for a homogeneous customer basis that we will extend to a setting with more than one customer class lateron.

In the second part (Chapters 4 - 6), we introduce stochastic processes as far as required for solving our model. We focus on Markov chains and here in particular on those with infinite state space. Ross (1983) and Wolff (1989) provide a more extensive account of Markov chain theory additionally covering reversible Markov chains. We first discuss the theory of Markov chains (Chapter 4) before we focus on their numerical solution (Chapter 5). In Chapter 6, we discuss stochastic ordering.

In the last part (Chapters 7 - 11), we present our results. In Chapter 7, we provide examples of situations with segmented customer basis. We introduce

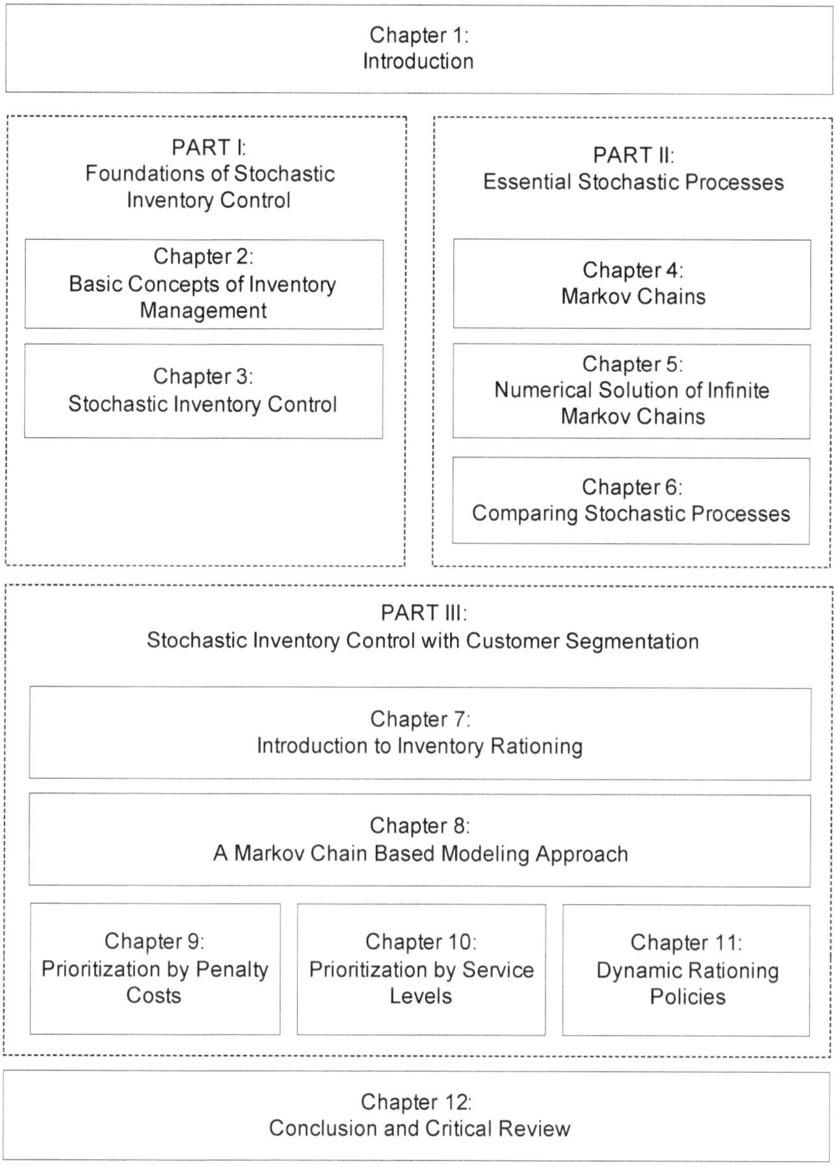

Figure 1.1: Structure of research

critical level rationing as one rule that has been studied to split inventory between different demand classes. We review the relevant literature and explain how our work fits in. Chapter 8 introduces our model and presents some basic results. In Chapter 9, this model is analyzed and optimized for the case of two customer classes prioritized based on the penalty costs caused by shortages. Chapter 10 treats the case of service levels instead of penalty costs. Up to this point, we have assumed that all parameters determining our control policy are constant over time. In Chapter 11, we develop some dynamic rationing policies and apply simulation to study their performance.

Chapter 12 concludes this thesis. We summarize the results and point out the major contributions of this research. In addition, we critically review the drawbacks and end with suggestions for future research.

Part I

Foundations of Stochastic Inventory Control

Chapter 2

Basic Concepts of Inventory Management

At the end of 2005, US-companies held inventories worth 1.41 trillion \$ or 11 % of the real GDP (Survey of Current Business, April 2006). This figure does not include governmental or non-profit organizations. Manufacturing accounts for 32 % of the inventory, wholesale for 22 % and retail for 28 %. The sum-in-itself already indicates the importance of inventory management. From a macroeconomic perspective, inventory movements have long been identified as dominant feature of business cycles (Abramowitz 1950). The analysis of the drivers has attracted microeconomic research, in particular modeling. But also for the single company, inventory management has increasingly gained attention as the widened scope of the subject shows.

In this chapter, we will discuss the scope and importance of inventory management (Section 2.1) and identify different motives for holding inventory (Section 2.2). In Section 2.3, we introduce different notions of inventory that are commonly distinguished in inventory management. We will then, in Section 2.4, identify the different cost factors associated with inventories. It is particularly difficult to quantify the cost incurred if we cannot deliver. Customers are disappointed, machines have to shut down for a while and production is delayed which might in turn lead to disappointed customers

K. Möllering, *Inventory Rationing*, Edition KWV,
https://doi.org/10.1007/978-3-658-24255-8_2

and many more aspects have to be taken into account. A means to circumvent these problems are service constraints that we are going to discuss in Section 2.5.

2.1 Inventory Management and Control

For a long time, inventory management was exclusively concerned with controlling inventories given a more or less stable supply, as e.g. Magee (1958) assumes in his treatment of the topic. In the mid-80s, the success of Japanese companies operating with far lower inventories than Western companies at that point of time illustrated two facts. Firstly, sophisticated inventory management can give a competitive advantage as capital not fixed in inventory can be invested elsewhere. And secondly, the operating conditions, such as delivery times, setup times and costs or quality defects, are not fixed but can be influenced (Silver et al. 1998). Consequentially, the scope of inventory management widened and now additionally comprises any inventory-related improvement effort, e.g. warehouse layout and quality management (Zipkin 2000). In this thesis, we will focus on inventory control in the classical sense, baring in mind that the traditional inventory models are also well-suited to analyze the impacts of improvements achieved by more general inventory-related initiatives.

The object studied in inventory control is referred to as *inventory system and* consists of a certain number of inventories linked by supply and demand processes (Zipkin 2000). A huge variety of arbitrarily complex inventory systems have been identified in the real world. In theory, inventory systems are typically classified by the number of items considered, the number of locations coordinated and the type of the system itself: There are single item and multiple items, single location and multiple locations and maybe multi-echelon[1], make-to-stock and make-to-order, distribution and assembly systems, to name a few (see e.g. Nahmias (2005) or Silver et al. (1998)).

Our focus for the remainder of this research will be on single item, single

[1] An echelon defines a certain stage in a supply chain. E.g. a supply chain consisting of a production facility, a wholesaler and a retailer, consists of three echelons (Nahmias 2005).

location, make-to-stock inventory system as displayed in Figure 2.1 with the difference that we will lateron divide the customer basis into different groups. However, the aspects outlined in this chapter hold for any inventory system.

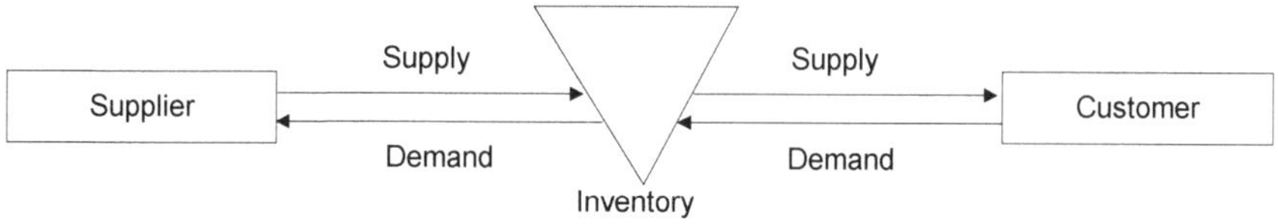

Figure 2.1: A simple inventory system

2.2 Motivations for Holding Inventory

Numerous motivations for holding inventory have been identified in the literature. The most cited ones include economies of scale, uncertainties in demand and supply, anticipated changes in demand and supply, decoupled processes, transportation, price and value speculations and inventory control costs (see e.g. Cachon and Terwiesch (2006), Nahmias (2005) or Silver et al. (1998)).

Economies of scale refer to the possibility to realize cost savings by producing or ordering in large quantities which are then kept as stock until they have been used. Producing or ordering large batches of one product allows for an amortization of fixed costs over a large amount of units (Nahmias 2005). Some production processes, e.g. bottling soft drinks (Thonemann 2005) or baking pasta products (Hammond 1994), require substantial investments in time, resources and money to switch from one product to another. Ordering full truckloads provides an answer to fixed setup cost incurred with each delivery as Cachon and Terwiesch (2006) explain.

Uncertainties may affect various aspects of a distribution system. Typically, the system is not flexible enough to respond to fluctuations in time (Zipkin 2000). Inventories are built up to prevent costly delays or shortages. The most important source of uncertainty is the demand. Ordering a new title, the bookseller has to forecast the amount he sells, he cannot be sure (Cachon and Terwiesch 2006). Demand for soft drinks might increase unexpectedly due to fine weather. Lead time, i.e., the time between ordering and order arrival, and quality of delivered goods are other sources of uncertainty that have attracted some attention in the literature.

Furthermore, *anticipation* of events influencing supply and demand might drive inventories. In contrast to uncertainties, anticipation refers to known or foreseen fluctuations in the supply and demand structure of an inventory system. Inventories now allow for a smooth production making optimal use of limited capacities and avoiding overtime (Silver et al. 1998). Shugan and Radas (2006) provide numerous examples of industries and services facing seasonal demand, e.g. due to weather conditions (demand for lighting products peaks in the winter) or annual events such as Christmas (retail industry). Prominent examples of seasonality on the supply side may be found within agriculture: Sugar beets are harvested during a short period of weeks only but processed during the whole year (Cachon and Terwiesch 2006). Other anticipated influences include large events such as the Olympic games (Shugan and Radas 2006) or escalating political crises in sourcing areas (Silver et al. 1998).

Decoupled processes form another motivation that stems from ensuring a smooth production flow. Of particular importance in serial production systems, decoupling allows to operate different stages of the production process independently. Buffer inventories prevent disruptions, e.g. because of tooling or breaks, that otherwise affected all other stages, both up- and downstream (Cachon and Terwiesch 2006), which could be very expensive (Fitzsimmons and Fitzsimmons 2005).

Transportation is also often named as a major motivation for holding inventories. Here, inventory relates to goods that have been ordered but have not yet arrived. As transportation requires time, orders do not arrive instantaneously. Thus this may also be seen as a mere necessity rather than a motivation. The amount of capital bound this way may be immense, especially if lead times are long (Nahmias 2005) and may only be lowered by reducing the lead times (Cachon and Terwiesch 2006).

A sixth motivation is *speculation*. If the price of a specific item is expected to rise in the future it might be beneficial to purchase additional inventory at the current, lower price (Nahmias 2005). Since China's steel demand increased sharply in 2003, steel prices have skyrocketed. A continued price increase from 290 $ in June 2003 to anticipated 650 $ per ton of hot-rolled coil steel in early 2005 (www.steelonthenet.com) might have lead companies to build up inventory. Similarly, inventory might be motivated by speculating on future value increases as it is the case with wines, cognacs or other alcoholic drinks.

Inventory control costs also motivate inventory as a minimum amount of stock requires carefully controlling the available amount of goods. Nahmias (2005) stresses that control costs form an important cost factor that is yet often overlooked. Inexpensive items, such as screws or nails, may not be worthwhile.[2]

2.3 Classification of Inventories

We have seen that companies hold inventory for various reasons. To obtain a better control of this inventory it is typically classified into different types. The classification itself depends on the perspective from which the inventory is looked at. The first (strategic) perspective distinguishes four types of inventory based on the value added at different stages of the manufacturing and processing. The second classification has a more operational background and divides the inventory based on their role within the inventory system for one or more specific goods within a specific strategic category.

2.3.1 The Strategic Perspective

In the context of manufacturing, the four types of inventory commonly distinguished from a strategic or - as Zipkin (2000) calls it - accounting perspective are raw materials, components, work-in-process (WIP) and finished goods (see e.g. Nahmias (2005)).

Raw materials are defined as resources required in the production or process-

[2] These items are often classified as C-items. For an introduction into the classification of goods into A-, B- and C-items we refer the reader to Bonini et al. (1997).

ing activity of a company. Items not having reached completion within the production process are referred to as *components*, also known as *sub-assemblies*. *WIP* relates to any inventory within the production process (Cachon and Terwiesch 2006). Nahmias (2005) stresses that this includes both, waiting inventory as well inventory that is worked on. Finally, the end products of a production process are known as *finished goods* and may be sold to customers without additional physical alteration.

Although in general, this also applies to distribution and services, Blinder and Maccini (1991) claim that those industries mainly stock finished goods. In manufacturing companies most inventory is locked up in raw materials that also account for the highest volatility in investments.

2.3.2 The Operational Perspective

From an inventory manager's point of view, inventories may be classified based on their role in the inventory system. This role may be based on the disposability or depend on the purpose.

When it comes to disposability, inventory can be either ordered, but not yet delivered (*pipeline stock* or *inventory on order*) or it is physically on the shelf (*on-hand inventory*). Silver et al. (1998) point out that inventory that is physically available may already be committed in some way, e.g. for demands of previous periods that have not yet been met, so called *backorders*. They refer to the remaining quantity as *net stock,* also known as *inventory level*, and it holds that

$$\text{net stock} \;=\; \text{on-hand inventory} \;-\; \text{committed / backorders.}$$

Since it does not make sense in a single-customer setting to hold both, on-hand inventory and committed inventory, for positive values the net stock coincides with the on-hand inventory and the amount of negative net stock equals the amount of committed inventory (see also Zipkin (2000) who explores this for backordering as the only means to commit inventory). The total disposable inventory is summarized in the *inventory position* that Silver et al. (1998) define as

$$\begin{aligned} & \text{inventory position} \\ = \; & \text{on-hand inventory} + \text{inventory on order} - \text{committed / backorders} \\ = \; & \text{net stock} \; + \; \text{inventory on order.} \end{aligned}$$

If the lead time is zero, then inventory position and net stock / inventory level coincide. As we will see in Section 3.2, the inventory position forms the basis for most ordering decisions.

The classification of inventories based on the purpose it serves within the inventory system is in some respects linked to the motivation of holding inventories discussed in the preceding section. Two types are typically distinguished to steer an inventory system: Cycle stock and safety stock. *Cycle stock* refers to the inventory that is produced or arrives in batches and is expected to be used (Cachon and Terwiesch 2006). On demand, stock is removed from inventory and the inventory gradually decreases until a new batch arrives which leads to the classic saw tooth inventory pattern (Bozarth and Handfield 2005). Cycle stocks are closely related to realizing economies of scale as these drive order or production batching. This relation is explored exemplarily in the deterministic economic order quantity model, a pure cycle stock model (Harris 1913). *Safety stock* finally refers to additional inventory kept to hedge against variabilities in demand and supply and as such motivated by various forms of uncertainty. It is quantified as the average inventory just before replenishment arrives (Silver et al. 1998).

Leenders (2005) states that cycle stocks may be found at any stage of the production process. This also holds for all the other types of inventory we just identified on the operational level. For instance, in a decoupled production process, the necessary buffer inventories also consist of cycle and safety stocks. Thus the operational classification may be regarded as a subclassification of the strategic classification. This relation is visualized in Figure 2.2.

The model, that we will develop takes the operational point of view.

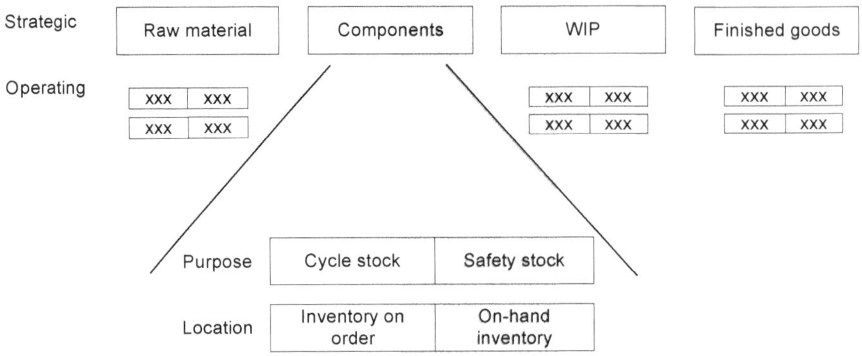

Figure 2.2: Types of inventory from different perspectives

2.4 Inventory-related Costs

Knowing the amount of stock for certain goods is essential for controlling and managing the inventory. But with inventory control cost as driver for inventory we also mentioned one factor indicating that the amount itself is not always the decisive measure. Callioni et al. (2005) emphasize even further that the correct accounting for the cost involved not only allows for improved inventory management but may even significantly influence managerial decisions, e.g. concerning the product portfolio. According to Nahmias (2005), all inventory-related costs belong to one of the following three categories: Order cost, holding cost and penalty cost. Similar classifications are used by Silver et al. (1998) and Lambert et al. (1998).

2.4.1 Order Cost

Order cost consists of fixed and variable cost components. The *fixed order* or *setup cost* includes all costs related to order generation, handling and bookkeeping. In a production context, changeovers require resources, e.g. special chemicals for cleaning or expert personnel. Cachon and Terwiesch (2006) additionally mention initial inefficiencies and scrap after a changeover. Furthermore, the time spent on the changeover could have been used for production and hence causes opportunity cost. Nahmias (2005) stresses the importance to distinguish clearly between fixed, but order-related, and overhead costs.

The price for which a product was purchased and its transport form the key drivers of the *variable order cost.* Initial order handling such as unwrapping and preparing it for sales or production often also rises proportional to the order size and should therefore be included in the variable order cost (Lambert et al. 1998). The variable order cost play a major role in calculating the holding cost.

2.4.2 Holding Cost

The term *holding cost* summarizes all costs associated with physically carrying inventory including for instance storage, packaging, control, salvaging and disposal, and is proportional to the inventory on hand at any point of time. Lambert et al. (1998) distinguish four different categories of such inventory-carrying costs: Opportunity costs, inventory risk costs, inventory service costs and storage costs.

Opportunity cost results from the capital fixed in inventory that could have been used for an alternative investment. Per item in stock and time unit, this cost can be determined by multiplying the variable order cost with an opportunity rate. Finding the correct opportunity rate constitutes a major problem: Commonly, the interest rate of return, return on assets and a company-specific hurdle rate[3] are used as a basis for calculating an opportunity rate. However, Silver et al. (1998) point out that this does not relate to realistic alternatives that may even vary in time. Zipkin (2000) warns that opportunity rates calculated using historic data may not be the right measure for the future. Also, opportunity rates should vary by product as some goods will be converted into (appropriate amounts of) cash more easily than others. But this may neither be practical nor necessary: In contrast to common textbook passages, Callioni et al. (2005) state that at Hewlett-Packard (HP) this cost component only accounts for 10 % of all inventory-carrying cost and has been outgrown by *inventory risk costs.*

[3] The hurdle rate indicates the minimum return on investment expected to actually pursue an investment (Nahmias 2005).

In this category, Lambert et al. (1998) list damage and deterioration, shrinkage, obsolescence and the cost associated with the risk of having to relocate goods in this category. They point out that - underestimating the effects of theft, poor records and spillage - especially shrinkage is frequently overlooked. Callioni et al. (2005) additionally name the risks of component devaluation, price protection and product returns. CPU's are a prominent example for speedy price deterioration that devalued massive inventories at HP. Price protection costs are incurred if the manufacturer drops the price for a product shortly after a distributor has purchased some inventory. The manufacturer might then be bound contractually to reimburse the partner for any item he still stocks. Product returns require rework and the manufacturer is once more exposed to the risk of devaluation during the reworking time. Price protection and product return risks affect manufacturers more than service companies.

Inventory service costs include taxes and insurances paid for stored inventory. Finally, *storage cost* is often named as holding cost item, but in many cases these costs are fixed. Plant or company-owned warehouses as well as the staff operating those belong to overhead. Thus, only storage in public or rented warehouses may be taken into account if the cost depends on the stock level.

2.4.3 Penalty Cost

Penalty or *shortage cost* refers to the cost incurred if there is not enough inventory to meet an actual demand. The actual cost components depend on the way, the stockout is handled. If a customer does not return, the contribution margin is lost (Lambert et al. 1998). Otherwise, companies face bookkeeping and administrative efforts as well as cost associated with a delayed delivery, e.g. some compensation for the waiting customer or express delivery charges. In a manufacturing context, emergency handling in reaction to stockouts, whether of finished goods or of raw materials, might additionally require rescheduling or splitting lots (Silver et al. 1998) or even a temporary closure of a production line due to missing resources (Nahmias 2005).

In both cases, negative publicity might lead to lost future sales, referred to as *loss-of-goodwill cost*. As Zipkin (2000) explains, a satisfying estimate for this intangible part requires market research and empirical studies and cannot be enforced for each and any item. Research by Walther (1996) concludes that one customer tells approximately nine other people about negative experiences.

Figure 2.3 gives a brief overview of all discussed cost categories.

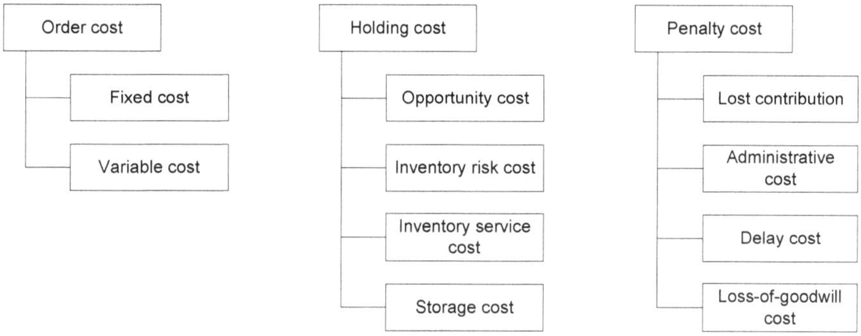

Figure 2.3: Categories of inventory-related costs

Some textbooks name *control cost* as fourth inventory-related cost category (e.g. Silver et al. (1998)). This cost relates to running an inventory systems and covers data acquisition, data storage, maintenance, training and so forth. However, these cost do not vary with the inventory level and may thus be considered as overhead.

2.5 Service Level

In the preceding section, we identified the different components that should be included in a penalty cost rate. As we have seen, some of those, such as loss of goodwill or the cost caused by delays, are rather intangible and difficult to quantify. A common means to circumvent these problems are service levels. In the one or the other way, service levels define certain probabilities to meet demand. Thus service levels determine a certain amount of security against the variabilities of demand (maybe taking into account fluctuations on the supply side) and determine a certain level of safety stock (Silver et al. 1998).[4] Most literature distinguishes α- and β-service levels.

The *α-service level*, also known as *in-stock probability* (Cachon and Terwiesch 2006) or *cycle service rate* (Silver et al. 1998), refers to the fraction of periods or cycles, in which no stockout occurs. Schneider (1981) points out that in continuous review settings, i.e., if the state of the system is observed permanently, this corresponds to the probability of no stockout during the lead time.

Brown (1967) introduced the *β-service level* or *fill rate*. This is defined as the proportion of demand that is immediately met from the on-hand inventory. The β-service level is often more appealing to practitioners as it additionally indicates the size of the problem (Silver et al. 1998), although Cachon and Terwiesch (2006) stress that it also depends on the business model which of the two service measures is more appropriate. A catalog retailer or a company depending on long lead times may be more interested in the fill rate while the grocery store wants to avoid stockout in general.

It is not always given that a high β-service level also implies a high α-service level and vice versa. However, in all cases an increase in the required inventory and thus in holding cost can be observed that is disproportionate to the required service levels (Thonemann 2005).

Silver et al. (1998) name a third service measure, the *ready rate* or *γ-service level*, that also takes into account the time of a stockout. It is defined as the proportion of time that he net stock is positive. This service measure has attracted comparatively little attention in the literature as determining the optimal inventory control policy under a γ-service level requirement is far more complex than under other service requirements. Application areas include mostly emergency equipment. In his study on the effect of different service levels on inventory control decisions, Schneider (1981) provides a comprehensive example that illustrates the difference between β- and γ-service level.

[4] This relation becomes particularly obvious when studying the basic stochastic inventory models for normally distributed demand. The interested reader is referred to Nahmias (2005) for a detailed treatment.

Chapter 3

Stochastic Inventory Control

If the demand is deterministic and we thus know exactly, how many units of a certain items will be demanded in a certain period, we just have to decide in how many chunks we order this quantity such that the holding costs and order costs are minimal. We may easily include quantity discounts or multiple products in our considerations. Zipkin (2000) treats various aspects of the so-called economic order quantity model for constant deterministic demand. Unfortunately, things become far more complicated, if some aspects are stochastic. For instance, weather conditions influence the shipping time of an order and might lead to damaged or spoiled goods. Thus not only lead time but also the yield of an order might be stochastic.

A special role plays the stochastic nature of demand. If demand is stochastic and can be arbitrarily high, we cannot avoid shortages completely (Silver et al. 1998). However, the expected amount of shortages depends on the order quantity. Although high order quantities may reduce the likelihood of shortages, they increase inventory on hand and thus holding cost. Therefore, the basic trade-off, not taking into account quantity discounts or fixed order cost, is between inventory holding and shortage costs.

In this chapter, we will give an overview of the most important factors that

K. Möllering, *Inventory Rationing*, Edition KWV,
https://doi.org/10.1007/978-3-658-24255-8_3

distinguish inventory models (Section 3.1). Despite of the range of imaginable settings there are four basic types of policies to control inventory in a stochastic setting. These types are presented in Section 3.2. The focus of this dissertation is on the mathematical optimization of an inventory system operating under a certain control policy, namely one that is closely related to the multi-period inventory control model. We will therefore study this model in detail in Section 3.3.

3.1 Characteristics of Inventory Models

Inventory control is typically concerned with two decisions: when to order and how much to order (Bonini et al. 1997). To optimize these decisions, a number of factors need consideration. Some of the attributes characterizing a certain inventory system offer alternatives that all have their pro's and con's. Those characteristics are discussed in Section 3.1.1. Other characteristics are more or less determined by the environment, at least temporarily. Those are discussed in Section 3.1.2.

3.1.1 Management Decisions

Fundamental choices concern the review pattern, the cost objective and the way in which shortages are considered. Those characteristics are not a result of a certain supply and demand structure but may be chosen freely. Also, there is no superior alternative. Either it is a pure management decision as in the case of the cost objective or the more accurate or thorough decision comes at a rate of increased cost and complexity and may thus be justified for certain items only.

- *Cost objective:* Traditionally, inventory models aimed at minimizing the long-run average or expected cost per period or time unit. More recently, the so-called *present value* or *discounted cost criterion* has gained some attention. The cost in period or time unit t are weighted with a factor $e^{-\alpha t}$ or $\frac{1}{(1+i)^t}$. This way, the financing aspect of investments is taken into account. In particular, this affects the inventory holding cost: Companies have to bridge the gap between purchasing and selling a good by borrowing money for which they pay a certain interest. Zipkin (2000) additionally points out that a unit in a warehouse does not generate linear interest charges as assumed in the average cost criterion. Thus the present value criterion is more accurate. Then again, the discounted cost criterion is criticized for leading to short-sighted decisions because it puts more weight on the near future than on the far future (Hayes and Garvin 1982).

- *Stockout Evaluation:* Companies sometimes prefer service constraints over penalty costs as the latter are difficult to determine. As a rule of thumb, Silver et al. (1998) suggest to take the hassle of determining penalty costs for very important items only. If service constraints are applied, then the type of service level has to be specified.

- *Review pattern:* Inventory control roughly distinguishes between *periodic* and *continuous review*. In a periodic review system, the inventory is monitored at certain discrete points in time only, typically with fixed time intervals between them. Actions such as ordering or delivery also take place periodically. In continuous review systems, on the other hand, information on the state of the system including the inventory is available at any point in time. The first approach facilitates coordination of different articles (Äxsater 2000). Especially, when handling a large amount of different items, this approach reduces complexity and cost as the inventory does not require continuous monitoring. The work is rhythmic and the workload rather predictable (Silver et al. 1998). On the other hand, continuous review allows for reduction of safety stock, as the time between two review periods does not need to be covered (Äxsater 2000).

3.1.2 System-Inherent Characteristics

In contrast to the management decisions of the preceding section, system-inherent characteristics result from the customer basis, the competitive situation and the whole structure of the supply and demand system. The most important ones include the nature of demand, the treatment of unfilled demand, lead time, yield and quality.

- *Demand:* Demand can vary in its predictability and its long-term behavior. Concerning predictability it is either deterministic or stochastic. Over time, it is either assumed to be constant or time-varying. While it is comparatively easy to incorporate time-varying demand in deterministic models (see Zipkin (2000)), Nahmias (2005) stresses that stochastic demand models rarely allow for non-constant demand rates. For practical purposes, deterministic demand may be assumed for basic, inexpensive items.

- *Excess demand:* If demand exceeds inventory, two extreme cases are commonly assumed: Either the customers wait patiently, e.g. because there is no alternative supplier, (complete backordering) or the customers will leave and fill their demands elsewhere (complete lost sales). Most practical situations see a mixture of the two extremes. Nevertheless, due to high service requirements in practice, the models assuming the one or the other extreme lead to similar solutions (Silver et al. 1998).

- *Lead time:* As demand, lead time may either be deterministic or stochastic. In the introduction to this section, we already mentioned weather as a cause for lead time uncertainty. The same holds for catastrophes and other exceptional situations. If production facilities, no matter if internal or external, are capacitated, the random demand suffices to induce random lead times (Zipkin 2000). Typically, larger or more variable lead times lead to higher optimal cost (Song 1994). Not including lead time variability can lead to a significant lack in service (Bagchi et al. 1986). However, including lead time uncertainty significantly increases complexity.

- *Yield or Quality:* As indicated weather conditions may spoil goods. Older machines not always produce the same quality. There are various reasons, why it cannot always be taken for granted that the replenishments contain the amount and the quality ordered. Inventory control distinguishes between deterministic (but not necessarily 100 %)

and stochastic yield. Yano and Lee (1995) provide an overview of the literature addressing this aspect.

Additionally, the number of products managed at once, the number of locations and the relevant cost factors, e.g. high or negligible setup cost per order, all have an influence on the "right" model for the decision maker.

3.2 Types of Inventory Control Policies

In Section 2.1, we defined inventory control as the theory concerned with managing inventory levels in a specific context. While there are multiple settings imaginable, the inventory policies all relate to four basic control policies regulating order timing and order quantities. If demand is deterministic and constant, optimal ordering occurs at regular time intervals and the size of the order is always the same (Zipkin 2000). For stochastic demand, this does no longer hold. In order to keep control policies simple to understand and implement, four different base types are distinguished that relax either the ordering at fixed time intervals or the fixed order quantity or both. Ordering at fixed time intervals relates to periodic review because information on the system between two orders is irrelevant.

Decisive for ordering decisions is always the inventory position, not the inventory level. For positive lead times, the inventory position takes into account the orders in the pipeline and avoids obsolete orders if for instance the inventory is empty but a huge replenishment will arrive shortly (Silver et al. 1998)

We will use the following notation (cf. Silver et al. (1998)): s reorder point, Q order quantity, R review period and S order-up-to level.[5] The most common continuous review policies, i.e., policies relaxing the fixed order intervals, are:

- *Fixed order quantity:* The control policy in this case is referred to as (s, Q)*-policy.* Whenever the inventory position reaches the reorder

[5] The order-up-to level is also referred to as base-stock level (Porteus 2002), the corresponding control policies as base-stock-level policies.

point s or drops below this point, an order of size Q is triggered. The reorder point r is supposed to optimize the risk of shortages. The policy corresponds to the mathematical model incorporating setup costs in addition to variable order, shortage and holding costs commonly attributed to Whitin (1957).

- *Variable order quantity:* The continuous review policy allowing for variable order quantities is the so-called *(s, S)-policy*. Under this policy, the size of the order - triggered whenever the inventory position reaches or drops below the reorder point s - equals the difference between the order-up-to level S and the current inventory position. If only unit demands occur, this is equal to a fixed order quantity of $S - s$. It can be shown that the service level under this policy can be significantly higher than under the (s, Q)-policy (Schneider 1979). Also, under this policy exceptionally large demands do not cause unreasonable risks. Nonetheless, the computational effort for finding the optimal parameters s and S is considerable. Furthermore, suppliers face variable orders which might increase lead time variability (Zipkin 2000). For $s = S - 1$, this policy is also called *one-for-one replenishment policy.*

Under periodic review, and thus ordering at fixed time intervals, the two basic policies both assume variable order quantities. They have been developed to respond to a certain cost structure. We therefore distinguish between the policy with and without fixed order costs.

- *Without fixed order cost:* For short, this policy is called the *(R, S)-policy*. The *review period* R indicates the length of the interval inbetween two reviews. At these points of time, the inventory position is observed and the difference between the inventory position and the order-up-to level S is ordered. This policy is most commonly used in practice despite the generally higher costs compared to a continuous review policy (see the detailed discussion in the previous section). By simply adjusting the order-up-to level, it allows fast reactions to changes in the demand pattern (Silver et al. 1998). Veinott (1965a) provides a proof of the optimality of this policy trading off shortage and holding costs (see Porteus (2002) for a more comprehensive outline).

- *With fixed order cost:* The policy, commonly referred to as (R, s, S)-*policy*, includes aspects of the (continuous review) (s, S)-policy in the (periodic review) (R, S)-policy: Every R intervals the inventory position is checked. An order is triggered only if the inventory position has reached or dropped below the reorder point s. Then the order size equals the difference between the order-up-to level S and the current inventory position. If fixed order costs are included in a periodic setting in addition to holding and penalty costs, this policy has been proven to be optimal (Scarf (1959) and Iglehart (1963)).

It is possible to argue for the one or the other policy looking at the cost factors considered. Table 3.1 gives a brief overview of the settings, under which the respective policies have been proven to be (close to) optimal.

Policy	Review		Costs			
	cts.	per.	variable	fixed	holding	penalty
(s, Q)	✓		✓	✓	✓	✓
(s, S)	✓		✓	✓	✓	✓
(R, S)		✓	✓		✓	✓
(R, s, S)		✓	✓	✓	✓	✓

Table 3.1: Basic inventory control policies and costs

However, fixed order quantities might also make sense in connection with certain means of transportation, e.g. full trucks (Zipkin 2000) or overseas containers (Silver et al. 1998).

3.3 Periodic Inventory Control

We will now study a periodic review system that operates under an (R, S)-policy. The model we are going to present in this section forms the foundation for our research and a lot of general aspects that we apply later originate here. Our goal is to optimize the order-up-to level S. Without loss of generality, we will assume a review period of 1 and will therefore suppress R henceforth. In a first step, we will consider a single-period model. We will then extend this model to a multi-period setting with instantaneous order arrivals. In a third step, we will introduce positive (constant) lead times and derive the optimal solution for the model with both, penalty costs as well as (α- and β-) service levels.

3.3.1 Single-Period Inventory Control

The stochastic nature of the demand leads to shortages or excess inventory depending on the inventory available at the beginning of a period. This inventory in turn depends on the order quantity. In the most basic setting, the optimal order quantity can be determined as the trade off between expected excess inventory and expected shortage cost. This model is also known as the *Newsvendor* or *Newsboy* model in reference to the news vendor who each day orders a certain quantity of the newspaper that sells during the day (Nahmias 2005). It can be traced back to Edgeworth (1888) and Arrow et al. (1951) and has seen multiple extensions covering random yield, multiple locations and many more. Khouja (1999) provides a comprehensive overview of these extensions. More detailed information may be found in Zipkin (2000).

The optimal order quantity S^* can be determined as follows: Assume that the distribution of the demand D is known. If the demand in the period exceeds the order quantity S, shortages are incurred that trigger underage or penalty cost. Else, inventory is left over and cost for excess inventory (underage cost) applies. The costs are all determined based on the situation at the end of the period. Let c_o and c_u denote the unit overage and underage cost respectively. Then the expected total cost at the end of the period ETC is[6]

$$ETC^S = c_o E[S - D]^+ + c_u E[D - S]^+$$

[6] We restrict the exposition to the for us important case of discretely distributed demand. All results in this first part carry over to continuously distributed demand with especially easy solutions in the case of normally distributed demand.

$$= c_o \sum_{d=0}^{\infty} \max(0, S-d) \Pr(D=d) + c_u \sum_{d=0}^{\infty} \max(0, d-S) \Pr(D=d)$$

$$= c_o \sum_{d=0}^{S} (S-d) \Pr(D=d) + c_u \sum_{d=S}^{\infty} (d-S) \Pr(D=d). \tag{3.1}$$

The cost function is convex in the order quantity S, which can be seen checking the second order difference equations (or derivatives in the continuous case). The interested reader is referred to Porteus (2002) for more detail. Consequentially, we obtain the minimum as the smallest order quantity S for which the first-order difference equation is greater than or equal to zero. Let F denote the cumulative distribution function (c.d.f.) of the demand. Then the optimal order quantity S^* is the smallest order quantity S such that

$$F(S) \geq \frac{c_u}{c_u + c_o}. \tag{3.2}$$

The fraction on the right hand side is often called the *critical ratio* (Nahmias 2005). It can be interpreted as an α-service level because the probability that the order quantity S covers the demand D of the period is higher than the critical ratio.

3.3.2 Multi-Period Inventory Control

The most basic extension of the newsvendor model to a multi-period setting assumes instantaneous order arrivals, i.e., the lead time is zero. This case as well as the case of positive lead time was also already covered by Arrow et al. (1951). Extensions and variations include lost sales, stochastic lead time, random yield, multiple items, multiple locations, and so forth. A couple of them may be found in Zipkin (2000). In this model, demands per period are assumed to be independent and identically distributed (i.i.d.). Unfilled demand of the previous period can be filled in succeeding periods (backordering) and inventory left over at the end of one period may be used to fill demands of future periods. Excess inventory at the end of a period now triggers holding cost of h per unit and period and backorders are penalized at a cost of p per unit and period. The order-up-to level S defines the target level for the inventory position (here the same as the inventory level) at the beginning of a period. Therefore, we obtain the order quantity Q_t by

$$S - IH_{t-1} + B_{t-1} = Q_t. \tag{3.3}$$

The inventory at the beginning of a period after ordering and order arrival then equals the sum of the order-up-to level S and, if applicable, backorders B_{t-1}. Therefore, the inventory on hand at the end of period t, IH_t, is $IH_t = [S - D_t]^+$. Similarly, the amount of backorders at the end of period t is given by $B_t = [D_t - S]^+$. As demands are i.i.d. the expected total cost as the end of a period does not depend on the period t and is thus equal to

$$\begin{aligned} ETC^S &= hE[S-D]^+ + pE[D-S]^+ \\ &= h\sum_{d=0}^{S}(S-d)\Pr(D=d) + p\sum_{d=S}^{\infty}(d-S)\Pr(D=d). \end{aligned} \tag{3.4}$$

As in Section 3.3.1, the cost function is convex in the order-up-to level S and the minimizing order-up-to level S^* is the smallest order-up-to level such that (Porteus 2002)

$$F(S) \geq \frac{p}{p+h}. \tag{3.5}$$

The following observation will be important for our research later on: At the end of period $t-1$, there is either inventory $IH_{t-1} = [S - D_{t-1}]^+$ or backorders $B_{t-1} = [D_{t-1} - S]^+$. In both cases, we obtain from Equation (3.3) that $Q_t = D_{t-1}$, i.e., in each period we order the demand of the previous period (see also Nahmias (2005)).

This pattern carries over to the case of a positive (constant) lead time LT. Thonemann (2005) provides a rigorous derivation of this. Again, the order-up-to level S is optimized. However, now the order-up-to level S does not directly control the inventory level, but the inventory position. The order quantity Q_t is therefore determined by

$$S - IO_t - IH_{t-1} + B_{t-1} = Q_t. \tag{3.6}$$

Again, our analysis does not depend on the specific period t. Arguing the same way as before, we obtain from Equation (3.6) that $IH = [S - IO - Q]^+ = [S - D^{LT+1}]^+$ and $B = [IO + Q - S]^+ = [D^{LT+1} - S]^+$ with D_{LT+1}

denoting the demand over $LT+1$ periods, i.e., $D^{LT+1} = \sum_{i=0}^{LT} D$. Now the expected total cost per period is

$$\begin{aligned} ETC^S &= hE[S - D^{LT+1}]^+ + pE[D^{LT+1} - S]^+ \\ &= h\sum_{d=0}^{S}(S-d)\Pr(D^{LT+1}=d) \\ &\quad +p\sum_{d=S}^{\infty}(d-S)\Pr(D^{LT+1}=d). \end{aligned} \tag{3.7}$$

and the optimal order-up to level S^* is equal to the smallest order-up-to level S such that

$$F_{LT+1}(S) \geq \frac{p}{p+h}. \tag{3.8}$$

F_{LT+1} denotes the c.d.f. of the demand over $LT+1$ periods, D^{LT+1}.

Figure 3.1 displays exemplarily the development of inventory level (net stock) and inventory position under this policy for an order-up-to level of $S^* = 15$ (data taken from Thonemann (2005)). We see, that the exact demand

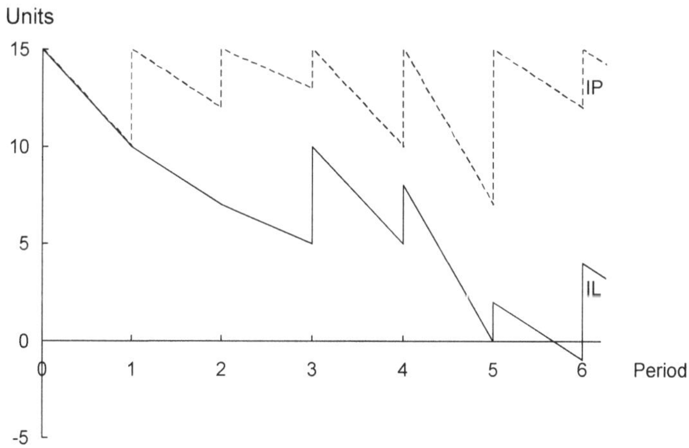

Figure 3.1: Inventory level and inventory position under (R, S)-policy

pattern within a period is not taken into account, only the inventory position at discrete time instances drives the ordering decision. A close look at the two lines reveals once again, that the order always coincides with the last observed demand.

3.3.3 Service-Constraint Multi-Period Inventory Control

To identify the optimal order-up-to level S^* requiring a certain α-service level instead of penalizing backorders with a cost charge, we solve the following minimization problem:

$$\begin{aligned} \min_S ETC^S &= h\, EIH^S \\ s.th.\ \Pr(B^S &= 0) \geq \alpha. \end{aligned} \tag{3.9}$$

In the multi-period setting with positive lead time, the probability that no backorders are incurred in a period is equal to the probability that the order-up-to level S is larger than or equal to the demand over $LT+1$ periods, D_{LT+1}. The expected inventory holding cost $h \cdot EIH^S$ are increasing in S. Thus we may reformulate Problem (3.9) as

$$\begin{aligned} &\min S \\ &s.th.\ F_{LT+1}(S) \geq \alpha. \end{aligned} \tag{3.10}$$

If a β-service level is imposed instead of an α-service level, the first question concerns the quantification of the β-service level. In the multi-period setting with lead time, the intuitive approach $1-\frac{EB^S}{ED}=\beta$ is only an approximation, as demand that has been backordered for more than one period is counted more than once (Thonemann 2005). However, for high service levels, the error will be small, as hardly any backorders will last for more than one period. The optimal order-up-to level S^* can thus be approximated as the solution of the following minimization problem

$$\begin{aligned} &\min S \\ &s.th.\ 1-\frac{E[D^{LT+1}-S]^+}{ED} \geq \beta. \end{aligned} \tag{3.11}$$

Hence S^* is the smallest order-up-to level S satisfying $E[D^{LT+1}-S]^+ \leq (1-\beta)\,ED$.

Part II

Essential Stochastic Processes

Chapter 4

Markov Chains

Stochastic inventory systems can usually be modelled as some kind of stochastic process: The inventory is a random variable that depends on the random demand, the expected lead time and yield of a replenishment, and the size of the outstanding and future replenishments. Mathematically, a *stochastic process* is a family of indexed random variables $\{X_t\}_{t \in T}$ that take values in a common state space $\Im$ (Ross 1983). We are only interested in stochastic processes with countable state space $\Im$ and we will assume that $T = \mathbb{N} = \{0, 1, 2, ...\}$.

In this chapter, we will study a very special kind of stochastic process, the Markov chain. We will introduce this stochastic process in Section 4.1. In particular we will focus on a certain subclass of Markov chains, namely those whose stochastic nature does not depend on $t \in T$. This class is defined in Section 4.2. If t tends to infinity, nice limit results hold that we will derive introducing the notion of communication classes (Sections 4.3 - 4.6). In Section 4.7, we will transfer our results to multi-dimensional Markov chains. Section 4.8 closes the chapter with some remarks on application areas.

K. Möllering, *Inventory Rationing*, Edition KWV,
https://doi.org/10.1007/978-3-658-24255-8_4

4.1 The Markov Property

Markov chains are the most popular kind of discrete stochastic processes. Precisely, they are defined as follows:

Definition 1 *(Krengel 2002, p. 195) Let* $\{X_t\}_{t\in T}$ *be a stochastic process with values in the countable state space* $\Im$*. It is a Markov chain, if the following condition (Markov property) is fulfilled:*
For all $t \in T$ *and all* $i_0, ..., i_t \in \Im$ *with* $\Pr(X_0 = i_0, ..., X_{t-1} = i_{t-1}) > 0$*, we have*

$$\Pr(X_t = i_t | X_0 = i_0, ..., X_{t-1} = i_{t-1}) = \Pr(X_t = i_t | X_{t-1} = i_{t-1}). \quad (4.1)$$

Equivalently, we may define a Markov chain as a stochastic process $\{X_t\}_{t\in T}$ satisfying for $t \in T, t \geq 1$

$$X_t = f_t(X_{t-1}, Z_t), t \geq 1 \quad (4.2)$$

with some functions f and r.v.s Z_t (Dümbgen 2003).

If we interpret X_t as the state of system in time period t, the probability of reaching a certain state in period t only depends on the state of the system in period $t-1$ and on $t-1$. It is not important how the state X_{t-1} has been reached. The inequality just assures that the conditional probability in Equation (4.1) is well-defined.

An example for a Markov chain is the following inventory system: Each period demand D_t occurs. The demands are independent. Unmet demand is lost. If there are less than s units left at the end of a period, Q units are ordered. Those orders arrive at the beginning of the next period. Let I_t denote the inventory at the beginning of a period after receiving orders, i.e.,

$$I_t = \begin{cases} [I_{t-1} - D_{t-1} + Q]^+ & \text{if } I_{t-1} - D_{t-1} < s \\ [I_{t-1} - D_{t-1}]^+ & \text{else.} \end{cases}$$

The family $\{I_t\}_{t\in T}$ then forms a Markov chain. However, if either demands were not independent or unmet demand was backlogged, the Markov property is no longer fulfilled. In those cases, the inventory I_t depends on older periods indirectly via the dependence of the demand or the backorders on previous periods. For more details on this example we refer the reader to Tijms (1994).

The conditional probabilities $\Pr(X_t = i_t | X_{t-1} = i_{t-1})$ are called *transition probabilities* (Wolff 1989). Applying the Markov property (4.1) and the relation between joint and conditional probabilities we obtain

$$\begin{aligned} & \Pr(X_0 = i_0, ..., X_t = i_t) \\ = \; & \Pr(X_0 = i_0) \Pr(X_1 = i_1 | X_0 = i_0) ... \Pr(X_t = i_t | X_{t-1} = i_{t-1}). \quad (4.3) \end{aligned}$$

The following equality, commonly known as *Chapman-Kolmogorov-Equation*, will be very useful for the determination of the limit distributions (Krengel 2002):
Let $\{X_t\}_{t \in T}$ be a Markov chain and $k < m < n$. Then for all $h, j \in \Im$ we have

$$\Pr(X_n = j | X_k = h) = \sum_{i \in \Im} \Pr(X_n = j | X_m = i) \Pr(X_m = i | X_k = h). \quad (4.4)$$

4.2 Homogeneous Markov Chains

So far, we have allowed the transitions probabilities to depend on and thus change with t. Of particular interest for us are Markov chains $\{X_t\}_{t \in T}$ where this is not the case, i.e., we require $\Pr(X_t = j | X_{t-1} = i) := p_{ij}$ for all $i, j \in \Im$ and all $t \in T$. Such Markov chains are called *homogeneous* or Markov chains *with stationary transition probabilities* (Krengel 2002). Using Equation (4.2), we obtain an alternative definition of homogenous Markov chains if we require that $f_t = f$ and that the r.v.s Z_t are i.i.d. for all $t \in T, t \geq 1$ (Dümbgen 2003). An example for a homogeneous Markov chain is the inventory system described in Section 4.1, because the demand distribution is the same in each period.

The matrix $P := (p_{ij})$ is called *transition matrix*. It is a stochastic matrix: By definition $p_{ij} \geq 0$, and by the law of total probability and Bayes' formula $\sum_{j \in I} p_{ij} = 1$ for all $i \in \Im$ (Ross 1983).

Homogeneous Markov chains are often visualized using knots as states and arrows as transitions. Figure 4.1 gives an example for such a visualization.

Figure 4.1: Example for a Markov chain

The transition probabilities p_{ij} describe the transitions between two succeeding states. Additionally, we may define the *n-step transition probability* $p_{ij}^{(n)} := \Pr(X_{t+n} = j|X_t = i)$. This probability does not depend on t. For $n = 1$, this is just the definition of the regular transition probabilities. For $n > 1$, it is a consequence of the Chapman-Kolmogorov-Equation (4.4) (Krengel 2002).

Let $P^{(n)}$ denote the n-step transition matrix of a Markov chain, i.e., the matrix with entries $p_{ij}^{(n)}$. Again by the Chapman-Kolmogorov-Equation (4.4), we have

$$p_{ij}^{(n+m)} = \sum_{k \in I} p_{ik}^{(n)} p_{kj}^{(m)}.$$

Thus $P^{(n+m)} = P^{(n)} P^{(m)}$ in the sense of matrix multiplication (Ross 1983).

Let $\pi_i^0 := \Pr(X_0 = i)$ for any $i \in \Im$. This *initial distribution* $\left(\pi_i^0\right)_{i \in \Im}$ and the transition matrix P uniquely determine the joint probabilities

$$\Pr(X_0 = i_0, ..., X_t = i_t) = \pi_{i_0}^0 \; p_{i_0 i_1} \; ... \; p_{i_{t-1} i_t} \tag{4.5}$$

(cf. Equation (4.3) and Krengel (2002)).

This leads to the question whether or not the long-term behavior of a homogeneous Markov chain depends on the initial conditions.

4.3 Limit Distribution and Invariant Distribution

To study the long-term behavior of Markov chains in more detail it is necessary to define the steady state as such.

Definition 2 *(Zheng 2005, p. 155) A distribution $\pi = (\pi_j)_{j\in\Im}$ is called a limit distribution w.r.t. the initial distribution $(\pi_j^0)_{j\in\Im}$ if for every $j \in \Im$, we have $\pi_j = \lim_{n\to\infty}\sum_k \pi_k^0 p_{kj}^{(n)}$. It is called the unique limit distribution if π_j is independent of the initial distribution, i.e., $\pi_j = \lim_{n\to\infty}\sum_k \pi_k^0 p_{kj}^{(n)}$ for any initial distribution $(\pi_j^0)_{j\in\Im}$.*

It is worth noting that if a unique limit distribution exists then for a fixed state k we obtain $\pi_j = \lim_{n\to\infty} p_{kj}^{(n)}$.

An existing (not necessarily unique) limit distribution may also be characterized in the following way: Let $\pi_j^n := \sum_k \pi_k^0 p_{kj}^{(n)}$. Then $\pi_j^{n+1} = \sum_k \pi_k^n p_{kj}$. Thus for the limit we have

$$\pi_j = \sum_{k\in\Im} \pi_k p_{kj} \tag{4.6}$$

and - as this is supposed to be a distribution -

$$\sum_{j\in\Im} \pi_j = 1. \tag{4.7}$$

If the state space is finite, the limit distribution is thus the left eigenvector of the transition matrix with eigenvalue 1.

Definition 3 *(Zheng 2005, p. 155) The non-negative solutions of the equation system (4.6) and (4.7) are called invariant distributions.*[7]

By definition, a limit distribution must be an invariant distribution. Uniqueness also transfers from limit to invariant distribution (Zheng 2005). The other direction does not hold as the following example illustrates: Averaging over time, both states of the Markov chain characterized by the transition matrix $\begin{bmatrix} 0 & 1 \\ 1 & 0 \end{bmatrix}$ are equally likely and $\pi = \left(\frac{1}{2}, \frac{1}{2}\right)$ is the unique invariant distribution. However, with initial distribution $\pi^0 = (1, 0)$, we obtain $\pi^{2n} = (1, 0)$ and $\pi^{2n+1} = (0, 1)$ for $n = 1, 2, ...$ Thus there is no limit distribution.

[7] *These distributions are sometimes also referred to as stationary, steady state or equilibrium distributions or invariant measure. Sometimes, these terms also refer to the limit distribution.*

4.4 Communication Classes

This section will introduce the concept of communication classes that will finally help us answer the questions concerning the long-term behavior of homogeneous Markov chains.

Definition 4 *(Ross 1983, p. 104) Let $\{X_t\}_{t\in T}$ be a homogeneous Markov chain. A state $j \in \Im$ is accessible from another state $i \in \Im$ if there is $n \geq 1$ such that the n-step transition probability $p_{ij}^{(n)}$ is positive.*

Visually, this means that it is possible to get from a state i to a state j following the arrows. For instance, in Figure 4.1 state 1 is accessible from state 3. Accessibility is a transitive relation, i.e., if j is accessible from i and k is accessible from j then k is accessible from i. This follows immediately from the Chapman-Kolmogorov-Equation (4.4).

If a state $j \in \Im$ is accessible from a state $i \in \Im$, this does not imply that i is also accessible from j. In the example above, state 3 is not accessible from state 1.

Definition 5 *(Ross 1983, p. 104) Two states that are accessible from each other communicate. If all states communicate, the Markov chain is called irreducible.*

Communication is an equivalence relation (Ross 1983) and the equivalence classes thus partition the state space. If all states communicate, i.e., if the Markov chain is irreducible, there is only one equivalence class.

Definition 6 *(Wolff 1989, p. 154) The set of states $j \in \Im$ that communicate is called a communication class.*

There are two communication classes in our example in Figure 4.1. The one consists of states 1 and 2, the other one of states 3 and 4. Thus the Markov chain is not irreducible.

4.5 Class Properties

Some very important properties of Markov chains either hold for all states of a communication class or for none. Those properties are therefore called *class properties* (Wolff 1989). In this section, we will introduce three essential class properties: Aperiodicity, Recurrency, and Transiency.

4.5.1 Aperiodicity

We consider paths that return to their starting state $i \in \Im$. The number of steps until a path returns to its starting state is called the *path length.*

Definition 7 *(Krengel 2002, p. 208) The greatest common divisor of the length of all those paths is the period. A chain with period 1 is called aperiodic.*

Note that we are not interested in "first" returns but allow unlimited visits to the state i. To illustrate this and the whole concept, we look again at the Markov chain characterized by the transition matrix $\begin{bmatrix} 0 & 1 \\ 1 & 0 \end{bmatrix}$: It is not possible to return to state 1 resp. 2 in an uneven amount of steps. Thus the period is 2.

Proposition 1 *(Ross 1983, p. 105) Aperiodicity is a class property.*

As an immediate consequence of Definition 7 and Proposition 1 the existence of a self-loop, i.e., $p_{ii} > 0$ for one $i \in \Im$, ensures the aperiodicity of the whole class.

4.5.2 Recurrency and Transiency

In this section, we will have an even closer look at returns. For $n \geq 1$, we define

$$f_{ij}^{(n)} = \Pr\{X_0 = i, X_n = j, X_k \neq j \text{ for } 1 \leq k < n\}.$$

Thus $f_{jj}^{(n)}$ is the probability to first return to a state j in n steps. The probability f_{jj} to return to the initial state j for the first time in an arbitrary amount of steps is thus defined as

$$f_{jj} = \sum_{n=1}^{\infty} f_{jj}^{(n)}.$$

Definition 8 *(Ross 1983, p. 105) A state $i \in \Im$ with $f_{jj} = 1$ is called recurrent. Otherwise, the state is called transient.*

Additionally, we define the expected return time m_{jj} as

$$m_{jj} = \sum_{n=1}^{\infty} n f_{jj}^{(n)}.$$

Definition 9 *(Ross 1983, p. 108) A recurrent state $j \in \Im$ is called positive recurrent if $m_{jj} < \infty$ and null recurrent otherwise.*

We also use the terms aperiodic, transient and (positive or null) recurrent for communication classes and Markov chains, if all states of a class or a Markov chain are aperiodic, transient, positive or null recurrent respectively.

Proposition 2 *(Wolff 1989, p. 154) Transiency, positive and null recurrency are class properties.*

We may link the expected return time of a state j to the limit probability of state j in the following way:

Proposition 3 *(Ross 1983, p. 108) Let i and j communicate. Then we have*

i. $\lim_{n\to\infty} \frac{1}{n} \sum_{k=1}^{n} p_{ij}^{(k)} = \frac{1}{m_{jj}}$.

ii. If j is aperiodic, then $\lim_{n\to\infty} p_{ij}^{(n)} = \frac{1}{m_{jj}}$.

iii. If j has period d, then $\lim_{n\to\infty} p_{ij}^{(nd)} = \frac{d}{m_{jj}}$.

Thus we may interpret the limit probability of a state j, if it exists, as the long-run period of time the chain spends in this state. Furthermore, an aperiodic state is positive recurrent if $\lim_{n\to\infty} p_{ij}^{(n)} > 0$ (Ross 1983).

4.5.3 Class Criteria

There are a couple of other useful properties to determine whether or not a class is positive or null recurrent or transient. The first four properties G1 - G4 are based on the fact that "open" communication classes, i.e., classes with at least one positive transition probability to a state outside this communication class, are always transient (Wolff 1989).

G1. *If it is possible to leave a communication class, this class is transient.*

G2. *It is not possible to visit a transient state from a recurrent state.* Otherwise, the transient state would be visited again in a finite number of steps as the chain has to return to the recurrent state again and again.

G3. *It is possible to access a recurrent state from a transient state.*

G4. *Starting in a recurrent state, the chain will never leave the class of this state.*

Thus a recurrent class in a way absorbs all probability mass. This behavior also explains the term "irreducible": A recurrent class acts like a small Markov chain because a chain that has entered this class will not leave it again and thus the long-run probability of all states outside this class will be zero. For the steady state analysis, we may thus reduce our attention to recurrent classes and treat each recurrent class as separate Markov chain. If the state space is finite, we can be sure that the one class of an irreducible Markov chain is recurrent. This is the content of Property F2 of the following list of properties that only hold for finite Markov chains (in reference to Zheng (2005)):

F1. *Not all states can be transient.* As the chain must visit somewhere infinitely often and there are only a finite number of states, at least one state must be recurrent.

F2. *All states of an irreducible finite chain are recurrent.* As there is at least one recurrent state and hence class in any finite Markov chain and there is only one class in an irreducible chain, this class must be recurrent.

F3. *Starting in a transient state, a finite chain will end up with some (not necessarily one) recurrent classes.*

F4. *All recurrent states are positive recurrent.* Starting in a recurrent class, the chain will never leave this class. Then the long-run proportion of time, that one state of this class is visited, is positive. Thus this state and therefore the whole class are positive recurrent.

Unfortunately, the Markov chain we use to model parts of our inventory system in the third part of this dissertation is not finite and thus lacks those nice properties.

However, the Markov chain displayed in Figure 4.1 is finite and we may thus use these properties to identify the transient and recurrent states: The chain has the two classes, $\{1, 2\}$ and $\{3, 4\}$. The first class is transient by Property G1. The second class is hence recurrent (Property F1).

4.6 Uniqueness of Limit Distributions

Finally, we will discuss the existence of a unique limit distribution of a Markov chain. The example in Section 4.5.1 already indicated that periodicity causes problems. If the Markov chain is irreducible and aperiodic, we obtain the following classification:

Theorem 1 *(Shiryaev 1996, p. 580) An irreducible, aperiodic Markov chain belongs to one of the following two classes:*

i. Either the states are all transient or all null recurrent. Then, $p_{ij}^{(n)} \to 0$ *as* $n \to \infty$ *for all* i, j *and there exists no limit distribution.*

ii. Or else, all states are positive recurrent. Then, $(\pi_j = \lim_{n\to\infty} p_{ij}^{(n)})_{j \in \Im}$ *is the unique limit distribution.*

Corollary 1 *A finite Markov chain admits a unique limit distribution if it is irreducible and aperiodic.*

If there are several recurrent classes, the long-term behavior usually depends on the initial state. By Properties G1 - G4, the choice of the initial state influences the probability that a certain recurrent class will be entered (Tijms 1994).

A Markov chain fulfilling the requirements of the second part of Theorem 1 is also referred to as *ergodic* (Ross 1983).

The first part of Theorem 1 implies that if a Markov chain is irreducible and aperiodic and there is a state with positive limit probability, then this state and thus the whole Markov chain can neither be transient nor null recurrent.

4.7 Multi-Dimensional Markov Chains

Although the states of all the examples mentioned so far were one-dimensional, this is no prerequisite. In this section, we will therefore provide an example of a Markov chain with two-dimensional states. The setting of the following example is adapted from Isaacson and Madsen (1976).

Consider the development of caries. Caries can be found in two different places: On one of the open surfaces of the tooth (dimension 1) or on the side between two teeth (dimension 2). There are three different stages a tooth can enter: Either it is healthy (0), it is decayed (1) or it is repaired (2). Thus we may describe the state of each tooth by a 2-tuple. A tooth in state $(0,0)$ is healthy, while a tooth in state $(1,2)$ has caries on the open surfaces and has been treated on its side. We can now assign these states to an indexed sequence $\{S_i\}$, c.g. $S_1 = (0,0)$, $S_2 = (0,1)$, ..., $S_5 = (1,1)$, $S_6 = (1,2)$. This way we can represent the transitions between the states in a common transition matrix, for instance of the following shape:

	S_1	S_2	S_3	S_4	S_5	S_6
S_1	*	0	0	0	*	0
S_2	0	0	*	0	0	0
S_3	0	0	*	0	0	*
S_4	0	*	0	0	*	0
S_5	*	0	0	0	0	*
S_6	0	*	0	0	0	0

Now we can proceed with the analysis as before.

4.8 Applications of Markov Chains

Applications of discrete-time Markov chains cover a broad range of problems. They are commonly applied in physics, particularly in statistical mechanics. Tijms (1994) gives examples in inventory control, communication theory and manufacturing. Other examples include Google's PageRank (Page et al. 1998) or the evaluation of monopoly strategies (Ash and Bischop 1972). More applications are available for continuous-time Markov chains (Tijms 1994). While the theory often treats them as separate objects, they are equivalent in a way: For any ergodic discrete time Markov chain there is a continuous time Markov chain with the same steady state probabilities and vice versa (Lal and Bhat 1988).

Related subjects such as hidden Markov chains, queuing theory or Markovian Decision Processes are widely applied in various scientific disciplines. Hidden Markov chains form the basis of speech recognition systems (Rabiner 1989). For Markov Decision Processes, White (1985) and White (1988) list numerous real world applications in areas as diverse as reacting to flood forecasts, determining research areas or revenue management.

Chapter 5

Numerical Solution of Infinite Markov Chains

In Section 4.3, we saw that for a finite state space, deriving the stationary distribution is equivalent to solving the following linear equation system:

$$\pi_j = \sum_{k=0}^{N} \pi_k p_{kj} \tag{5.1}$$

and

$$\sum_{j=0}^{N} \pi_j = 1. \tag{5.2}$$

There are numerous algorithms for solving such an equation system numerically and we will present some in Section 5.3. Often, the distribution may even be derived analytically. However, if the state space is infinite, the set of equations to solve is infinite and analytical solutions are less likely. Sometimes it might be possible to derive the limit distribution or at least the long-run expectation using generating functions (Wolff (1989) gives a brief introduction to this approach). Otherwise, the Markov chain has to be solved numerically.

Two general approaches may be distinguished for infinite Markov chains: System reduction approaches make use of special properties of the transition

K. Möllering, *Inventory Rationing*, Edition KWV,
https://doi.org/10.1007/978-3-658-24255-8_5

matrix or the steady state distribution in order to solve the infinite equation system (4.6) and (4.7). State space reductions only take into account a finite number of states. Both approaches finally apply solution algorithms developed for finite state Markov chains resp. finite linear equation systems.

In this chapter, we will provide an overview of those numerical solution methods. Section 5.1 discusses system reduction approaches whereas Section 5.2 focuses on methods reducing the state space of the system. Some algorithms are presented Section 5.3. The chapter closes with a collection of criteria with which a suitable algorithm might be identified (Section 5.4).

5.1 System Reduction Approaches

The matrix-geometric solution approach of Neuts (1995) - originally developed for efficiently solving finite linear equation systems - formed the basis for the development of solution approaches other than brute-force state space cut-offs. While most of these algorithms are based on so called reduced systems, Section 5.1.2 gives an example for another way to reduce the equation system to a finite one.

5.1.1 Reduced System Approaches

Lal and Bhat (1988) give an overview of these approaches. They outline the general idea of a reduced system approach as follows: Let P denote the transition matrix and let M denote the matrix $P-E$ with E the unit matrix. Let $\underline{1}$ denote the vector with all entries equal to 1. Then the equation system (4.6) and (4.7) may be rewritten as

$$\pi M = 0 \text{ and } \pi \underline{1} = 1. \tag{5.3}$$

Now assume that M is partitioned as follows

$$M = \begin{bmatrix} A & B \\ C & D \end{bmatrix}$$

and B is invertible. Partitioning the vectors π and $\underline{1}$ accordingly, we may rewrite Equations (5.3) as

$$\pi_1 A + \pi_2 C = 0,\ \pi_1 B + \pi_2 D = 0 \text{ and } \pi_1 \underline{1}_1 + \pi_2 \underline{1}_2 = 1.$$

This system can be transformed to

$$\pi_1 = -\pi_2 D B^{-1} \tag{5.4}$$

and

$$\pi_2 (C - DB^{-1}A) = 0 \text{ and } \pi_2(\underline{1}_1 - DB^{-1}\underline{1}_2) = 1. \tag{5.5}$$

Equations (5.5) are referred to as the *reduced system*. They allow us to determine π_2. With this knowledge, we may then use Equation (5.4) to solve for π_1.

If the system is infinite, Lal and Bhat (1988) require the matrix B to be standard, i.e., each diagonal entry of the sub-matrix B is assumed to equal a diagonal entry of the original matrix M. In this case, matrix-analytical consideration lead to a finite reduced system.

5.1.2 Geometric Tail Distributions

Based on a certain behavior of the tail of the steady state probabilities, Tijms and van de Coevering (1991) reduce the infinite equation system (4.6) and (4.7) to a finite one and apply the usual solution algorithms (see Section 5.3) to this finite linear equation problem.

Definition 10 *(Tijms 1994, p. 119) A distribution $(p_j)_{j \in \mathbb{N}}$ has a geometric tail if there exist constants η and γ, $0 < \eta < 1$, $\gamma > 0$, such that $p_j \approx \gamma \eta^j$ for all $j > j'$ and j' sufficiently large.*

For our purposes here it suffices to determine the constant η which can be computed rather easily using generating functions (Tijms 1994). Assuming such a behavior for the steady state distribution π of an infinite Markov chain, we obtain

$$\lim_{j \to \infty} \frac{\pi_{j+1}}{\pi_j} = \eta.$$

Thus for $j \geq M$, we may express the steady state probabilities π_j by

$$\pi_j = \pi_M \eta^{j-M}.$$

With this, the infinite equation system (4.6) and (4.7) becomes

$$\pi_j = \sum_{k=0}^{M-1} \pi_k p_{kj} + \sum_{k=M}^{\infty} \pi_M \eta^{k-M} p_{kj} \text{ for } j = 0, ..., M-1 \tag{5.6}$$

and

$$\sum_{k=0}^{M-1} \pi_k + \frac{\pi_M}{1-\eta} = 1 \tag{5.7}$$

where we made use of the convergence of the geometric power series, i.e., $\sum_{k=M}^{\infty} \eta^{k-M} = \frac{1}{1-\eta}$. Equations (5.6) and (5.7) form a finite equation system and can be solved easily.

5.2 State Space Reduction Approaches

If a positive recurrent infinite Markov chain will be solved by reducing the state space to a finite one (truncation), there are some aspects that have to be taken into account: Firstly, the truncated transition matrix has to be turned into a stochastic matrix in order to apply the finite Markov chain algorithms. Secondly, this new transition matrix has to approximate the infinite matrix well. Independent of the size of the truncated transition matrix - that also plays a role - this is not always the case (Tweedie 1998). In this section, we will first provide some augmentation methods and will then discuss specific criteria that ensure convergence of the truncated steady state probabilities against the original ones.

5.2.1 Augmentations

There are various ways to truncate a matrix. The most intuitive truncation is the so-called *Northwest truncation* which considers only the entries in the Northwestern corner of the original transition matrix (Seneta 2006). But independent of the choice of states taken neglected for further analysis, the resulting truncated transition matrix is sub-stochastic. The procedure to turn the truncated matrix into a stochastic matrix, a prerequisite of most solution algorithms, is called *augmentation.* For one-dimensional Markov chains, the most common augmentation methods are (see for instance Zhao and Liu (1996)):

- *First Column Augmentation:* The first entry in each row is changed in such a way, that the row sum equals 1 again, i.e.,

$$p_{i0} = 1 - \sum_{j=1}^{N-1} p_{ij}.$$

- *Last Column Augmentation:* Instead of the first entry the last entry in each row is changed in such a way, that the row sum equals 1 again, i.e.,

$$p_{iN-1} = 1 - \sum_{j=0}^{N-2} p_{ij}.$$

- *Censoring (Watching):* This method divides the original infinite state space into a set E and its complement E^C. Basically, we now construct the transition matrix for the stochastic process that can be observed in E. Thus we only *watch* the sample paths while they move from within E and *censor* the parts in E^C. For more details the reader is referred to Freedman (1983) who also points out that in general it is not easy to compute the censored transition matrix from the original one.

Other methods include for instance hybrid approaches, augmenting other columns or augmenting different entries in each row.

Assuming convergence of the invariant distribution of the truncated transition matrix against the invariant distribution of the original transition matrix, we would like to minimize the error we make by augmentation. Suitable measures are the ℓ_1- norm measuring the error sum,

$$\ell_1(N, \infty) = \sum_{j=0}^{N-1} \left|\pi_j^N - \pi_j\right| + \sum_{j=N}^{\infty} \pi_j,$$

and the ℓ_∞- norm measuring the maximum error,

$$\ell_\infty(N, \infty) = \max\left\{\max_{0 \leq j < N} \left|\pi_j^N - \pi_j\right|, \max_{j \geq N} \pi_j\right\}.$$

For a long time, last column augmentation was assumed to be best while the first column augmentation was known to perform poorly (Zhao et al. 1999). Only recently, Zhao and Liu (1996) proved the following properties assuming Northwest truncation:

Proposition 4 *(Zhao and Liu 1996)*

1. *Censoring is an augmentation method that minimizes the error sum* $\ell_1(N, \infty)$.
2. *If the original transition matrix is upper Hessenberg ,i.e.,* $p_{ij} = 0$ *for all* $i > j + 1$*, then last column augmentation leads to the same error sum* $\ell_1(N, \infty)$ *as censoring.*
3. *Censoring might be superior to last column augmentation with respect to the maximum error* $\ell_\infty(N, \infty)$.

In the multi-dimensional case, we can of course apply the same augmentation methods as before since we mirror all transitions in a standard transition matrix (see Section 4.7). Proposition 4 remains valid as Zhao and Liu (1996) assume a standard Northwest truncation mainly for indexing purposes. However, there are augmentation methods that take into account specific structures of the transition matrix. If the matrix is block-structured, Zhao and Liu (1996) for instance also names

- *Last Column Block-Augmentation:* Let $P = (P_{ij})$ be a stochastic matrix with mxm-submatrices P_{ij} and assume that the truncated matrix includes the first N of those matrices. Then the last block takes the same role as the last entry in each row in the Last Column Augmentation but obeying by the block structure of the matrix, i.e.,

$$P_{iN-1} = 1 - \sum_{j=0}^{N-2} P_{ij}.$$

5.2.2 Pointwise Convergence

Let us now assume that the transition matrix of an infinite positive recurrent Markov chain with only one closed class has been truncated applying

Northwest truncation. Note that this Markov chain, even though it may be periodic, has a unique invariant distribution, but not a unique limit distribution (Zheng 2005). Let P^N denote the truncated transition matrix and $\overline{P}^N$ a stochastic matrix of the same size with $\overline{p}_{ij}^N \geq p_{ij}^N$ for all i, j. Let $\left(\pi_j^N\right)_{j\in\Im}$ denote the invariant distribution of $\overline{P}^N$. A priori, this distribution $\left(\pi_j^N\right)_{j\in\Im}$ converges against the invariant distribution $(\pi_j)_{j\in\Im}$ of the original Markov chain in the following sense :

$$\lim_{N\to\infty} \frac{\pi_j^N}{\pi_k^N} = \frac{\pi_j}{\pi_k},\ j, k \in \mathbb{N}.$$

In this section, we will discuss conditions under which pointwise convergence may be established, i.e.,

$$\lim_{N\to\infty} \pi_j^N = \pi_j,\ j \in \mathbb{N}.$$

Proposition 5 states that when truncating transition matrices of ergodic infinite Markov chains, pointwise convergence is achieved independent of the applied augmentation.

Proposition 5 *(Gibson and Seneta 1987) Let P denote the transition matrix of an ergodic infinite Markov chain and P^N the Northwest-truncated transition matrix. Let $\overline{P}^N$ be a stochastic matrix of the same size with $\overline{p}_{ij}^N \geq p_{ij}^N$ for all i, j. Then for sufficiently large N, $\overline{P}^N$ admits a unique invariant distribution $\left(\pi_j^N\right)_{j\in\Im}$ and $\lim_{N\to\infty} \pi_j^N = \pi_j$, $j \in \mathbb{N}$.*

Defining $\overline{P}^N$ as the augmented truncated transition matrix, the prerequisites of this proposition are fulfilled. It does not matter which augmentation is applied. Gibson and Seneta (1987) show the same result for upper-Hessenberg matrices.

It is not always the case that any augmentation leads to the desired convergence. Tweedie (1998) proves pointwise convergence for matrices with a specific property for last column augmentation only. The required property is stochastic monotonicity.

Definition 11 *(Tweedie 1998) A Markov chain is stochastically monotone if its transition matrix P with entries p_{ij} is positive recurrent and for every i, j with $i < j$, we have $\sum_{m>k} p_{im} \leq \sum_{m>k} p_{jm}$ for every $k \in \mathbb{N}$.*

Proposition 6 now states that this monotonicity ensures convergence given last column augmentation.

Proposition 6 *(Tweedie 1998) Let $\overline{P}^N$ be the Northwest truncated transition matrix augmented in the last column. If a Markov chain is stochastically monotone, then*
$\lim_{N\to\infty} \left\|\pi^N - \pi\right\| = \lim_{N\to\infty} \sum_j \left|\pi_j^N - \pi_j\right| = 0.$

Other conditions are known that lead to the same pointwise convergence. Li and Zhao (2000) introduce *stochastic block-monotonicity.* Others may for instance be found in Tweedie (1998) and Seneta (2006).

5.3 Algorithms

As already mentioned, a huge variety of algorithms are available for solving finite Markov chains. There are direct approaches such as Gauss elimination and the GTH-algorithm (Grassmann et al. 1985). Unfortunately, those approaches mostly require the whole coefficient matrix to be stored and updated and applications is hence often limited by storage capacities (Barge 2002). Other approaches allow for a more efficient storage skipping all zero-elements. They can be clustered as iterative methods, e.g. vector iteration or Gauss-Seidel Iteration, projection or decomposition methods. The reduced system methods of Section 5.1.1 are also applicable. Bylina and Bylina (2004) and Philippe et al. (1992) provide brief overviews of the available numerical methods. For details and a thorough analysis of the algorithms, the reader is referred to Stewart (1994). In this section, we will exemplarily discuss the two approaches we used in our numerical analysis.

5.3.1 Sheskin's Partitioning Algorithm

An exact algorithm for aperiodic, irreducible, finite Markov chains like ours (after truncation) is the partitioning algorithm of Sheskin (Sheskin 1985). This algorithm repeatedly partitions the transition matrix creating a sequence of smaller transition matrices. The components of the steady state probabilities are then computed starting from the smallest transition matrix.

Algorithm 1 The algorithm runs as follows (Merlo et al. 1996):

for $n = N - 1$ to 1 do

$H = \sum_{j=0}^{n-1} p_{nj}$

for $i = 0$ to $n - 1$ do

$p_{in} = \frac{p_{in}}{H}$

endfor

for $i = 0$ to $n - 1$

for $j = 0$ to $n - 1$

$p_{ij} = p_{ij} + p_{in} p_{nj}$

endfor

endfor

endfor

$\sigma = 1$, $r_1 = 1$

for $j = 1$ to $N - 1$ do

$r_j = \sum_{k=0}^{j-1} r_k p_{kj}$

$\sigma = \sigma + r_j$

endfor

for $j = 0$ to $N - 1$ do

$\pi_j = \frac{r_j}{\sigma}$

endfor

Since it does not contain any subtractions, Sheskin's algorithm is stable and rather resistant to rounding errors even if the underlying transition matrix is ill-conditioned (Grassmann 1993). Except for storage space, it does not incorporate any limitations to the size of the transition matrix and is therefore well-suited for our purposes. It is however a direct approach. Merlo et al. (1996) show that it is basically the same as the GTH-Algorithm. Although - unlike other direct approaches - the algorithm only requires storing one column vector of the transition matrix and each reduced matrix, storage requirements are still considerable.

5.3.2 Power Iteration

This iterative approach is the most intuitive one. We again assume that the Markov chain is irreducible and aperiodic. We repeatedly apply the transition matrix P to an arbitrary initial distribution vector x. The iteration is thus of the form (Bylina and Bylina 2004)

$$x^{(k+1)} = P^T x^{(k)}.$$

For $k \to \infty$, the iteration converges against the solution of Equation (4.6). Since the row sums all equal 1 and the eigenvalue is 1, the solution we obtain automatically fulfills Equation (5.1) and Equation (5.2) and is thus the unique invariant distribution we looked for.

Depending on the ratio of the subdominant eigenvalue λ_2 to the dominant eigenvalue 1, convergence can be very slow. This is for instance the case if the matrix is nearly completely decomposable, i.e., if the state space may be decomposed into parts with strong interactions inbetween and weak interactions to other parts (Philippe et al. 1992).

5.4 Criteria for Choosing a Specific Algorithm

As we will see in the third part of the thesis, the selection of an algorithm in our case was not too difficult: The transition matrix of our Markov chain did not fulfill any of the prerequisites for the more sophisticated approaches. In general, the choice is not easy and even subject to scientific research. The criteria that Barge (2002) lists can be divided into two groups. On the one hand, there are limitations to the applicability of algorithms due to the transition matrix, such as

- Matrix structure
- Closeness of the matrix structure to some exploitable form
- Sparseness of the matrix
- Matrix size (and storage possibilities).

On the other hand, there are often requirements and trade-offs for the solution that are often related to convergence rate, e.g.

- Time for finding a solution
- Accuracy of the solution.

For more details, we refer the reader to Barge (2002).

Chapter 6

Comparing Stochastic Processes

In our work we are not only interested in a specific Markov chain but we also want to compare different Markov chains w.r.t. to their long-term behavior. Different ordering relations have been studied that also incorporate additional information such as convexity (Stoyan 1983). We will only be interested in the simple ordering of cumulative distribution functions.

In this chapter, we will introduce this stochastic ordering relation (Section 6.1). In Section 6.2, we will provide a powerful method to compare different random variables and processes.

6.1 Stochastic Ordering for Distribution Functions

We would often like to compare r.v.s in a way similar to deterministic numbers. However, we cannot simply compare random realizations but have to take into account the stochastic nature. Definition 12 introduces an ordering that transfers the common notions of some number being greater or smaller than and equal to another number to stochastic context.

K. Möllering, *Inventory Rationing*, Edition KWV,
https://doi.org/10.1007/978-3-658-24255-8_6

Definition 12 *(Stoyan 1983, p. 4) Let X and Y be r.v.s defined on the same probability space with c.d.f.s F and G. Then X is stochastically smaller than Y, if F and G satisfy*

$$F(x) \geq G(x) \text{ for all } x.$$

We write $X \leq_{st} Y$.

The relation *stochastically larger* may be defined analogously. The relation $\leq_{st}$ defines a partial ordering, i.e., it is reflexive, transitive and antisymmetric (Stoyan 1983).

By Definition 12, the smaller r.v. X is distributed in such a way, that small realizations are more likely than small realizations of Y. Thus for non-negative r.v.s it is intuitively clear that $X \leq_{st} Y$ implies $EX \leq EY$. Proposition 7 states that this holds in general.

Proposition 7 *(Stoyan 1983, p. 6) For any r.v.s X, Y with $X \leq_{st} Y$,*

$$EX \leq EY.$$

Note, that $EX \leq EY$ may also hold for r.v.s without $X \leq_{st} Y$. For example, let X and Y be r.v.s that may take the values 0, 1 and 2. Table 6.1 displays the density functions of the two variables.

i	$\Pr(X = i)$	$\Pr(Y = i)$
0	0.4	0.5
1	0.5	0.2
2	0.1	0.3

Table 6.1: Distribution of variables X and Y

Then neither $X \leq_{st} Y$ nor $X \geq_{st} Y$, but $EX \leq EY$.

Often we do not directly consider r.v.s X and Y, but are interested in functions of those.

Proposition 8 *(Ross 1983, p. 252) Let X and Y be r.v.s defined on the same probability space. Then*

$$X \leq_{st} Y \iff E[f(X)] \leq E[f(Y)]$$

for all nondecreasing functions f.

As an immediate consequence, stochastic ordering is for instance preserved under application of the maximum-operator or under summation.

The next property will be of fundamental importance to us: Under certain circumstances, we may derive the steady state relation of two stochastic processes from the relation in the single periods.

Proposition 9 *(Stoyan 1983, p. 6) The relation $\leq_{st}$ has the weak convergence property: Let $\{X_n\}$ and $\{Y_n\}$ be r.v.s with c.d.f.s $\{F_n\}$ and $\{G_n\}$ that converge weakly against the c.d.f.s F and G of r.v.s X and Y. If $X_n \leq_{st} Y_n$ for all n, then also $X \leq_{st} Y$.*

6.2 The Sample Path Method

This section introduces a method that we will use over and over again in order to compare stochastic processes.

Definition 13 *(Wolff 1989, p. 54) Let $\{X_t\}_{t\in T}$ be a stochastic process on a probability space $(\Omega, \Pr)$. For a fixed $\omega \in \Omega$, the stochastic process is a function of the index t and is called sample path of the process.*

We may now study those sample paths to directly compare two stochastic processes.

Proposition 10 *(Wolff 1989, p. 485 f.) Let $\{X_t\}_{t\in T}$ and $\{Y_t\}_{t\in T}$ be two stochastic processes defined on the same probability space $(\Omega, \Pr)$. Then for fixed $t \in T$*

$$X_t(\omega) \leq Y_t(\omega) \text{ for all } \omega \in \Omega \;\Rightarrow\; X_t \leq_{st} Y_t.$$

Proposition 10 is a special case of Kamae et al. (1997) who also proved the opposite direction. Obviously, the condition on the left hand-side, $X_t(\omega) \leq Y_t(\omega)$ for all $\omega \in \Omega$, is stronger than the condition in Definition 12. Thus to prove a certain stochastic ordering of the long-term behavior of two stochastic processes in the sense of Definition 12, it suffices to show the following three aspects:

1. The stochastic process converges weakly in the sense of Proposition 9.

2. For *each* $t \in T$, *each* sample path fulfills the condition of Proposition 10.

It is worth noting that this method assumes a common probability space $(\Omega, \Pr)$ for the two r.v.s X_t and Y_t. If this is not given, one might construct two r.v.s with the same stochastic behavior as the original ones but based on the same random influence, i.e., using the same probability space, and compare the newly constructed r.v.s. This method is called *stochastic coupling*. As our application does not require stochastic coupling we refer the reader to Ross (1983) for a brief outline and Lindvall (2002) for more details.

Part III

Stochastic Inventory Control with Customer Segmentation

Chapter 7

Introduction to Inventory Rationing

In competitive markets, customer differentiation is becoming increasingly important. For instance, companies offer special services to customers who are willing to pay more. Inventory control has to ensure that those extra-ordinarily high requirements are met. A simple way would be to increase inventory to a level that guarantees a high service standard for all customers. Alternatively, inventory control can take into account the inhomogeneous customer basis and - if necessary - reserve stock exclusively for important customers. We will refer to such an approach as *inventory rationing*. Nahmias and Demmy (1981) show that inventory rationing enables a company for instance to offer a significantly higher service level for high priority customers without increasing the order-up-to level S. For a single-period model with two customer classes, both with exponentially distributed demands ($\lambda_1 = \lambda_2 = 0.1$), and assuming an order-up-to level of 50, they calculate an increase in the β-service level for high priority customers from 97.6% to 99.3% solely due to the fact that class 2 customers are only served once serving of class 1 customers has been finished. Given that those high priority customers are willing to pay an additional fee for the improved service, this in turn increases profits.

K. Möllering, *Inventory Rationing*, Edition KWV,
https://doi.org/10.1007/978-3-658-24255-8_7

In this chapter, we will provide several examples to underline the growing importance of inventory rationing (Section 7.1). Situations with inventory demanded by several customer groups also occur in other research areas, namely in revenue management and multi-echelon systems. Thus, in Section 7.2, we will briefly discuss similarities and fundamental differences. In Section 7.3, we will indicate the wide range of rationing methods applied and studied. The analysis of these rationing policies is complicated by backordering. In particular, under periodic review the question occurs when to clear which backorders. Section 7.4 explores the role of backorders and potential backorder clearing mechanisms. This section is followed by the literature review (Section 7.5). In the final Section 7.6 we indicate how our work fits with the existing research.

7.1 Examples for Different Customer Classes

An example from the service-parts division of a major European mobile telephone company shows that penalty costs can differ significantly. At the company, some service parts are used at different levels of the telecommunication network, for instance in antennas and network computers. If a part fails in an antenna, the antenna goes down. If the same part fails in the network computer, the network computer goes down and about 30 antennas become unavailable. Thus the failure of this part in the network computer causes about 30 times higher penalty cost than in the antenna. In situations like this it is beneficial to classify demands according to their penalty costs and treat different demand classes differently. The customer classes in this example are a result of common components. This strategy has been increasingly adopted, e.g. in the context of mass customization and postponement, to adjust to shrinking product lifecycles and product variety proliferation (Swaminathan and Lee 2003).

In other situations, customer segmentation might be due to contractually agreed service levels. Kleijn and Dekker (1998) describe such an application in the airline industry: A company provides spare-parts for aircraft. With several airlines the company is contractually bound to supply the desired part within 24 hours in 95 % of the cases. From time to time, other airlines also request parts and the company has to decide if they sell the desired part or keep it to be able to meet the service standards agreed with their main customers.

Very similar to this example is the situation of a glass manufacturer as outlined by Frank et al. (2003). This company provides the big Detroit-based car manufacturers with windscreens etc. but also faces demand from the after-market. However, the contracts with the car manufacturers require just-in-time deliveries and high penalties for late or missed deliveries.

Deshpande et al. (2003) provides an example from the US military. For their service parts, the different military services, i.e., navy, army and air-force, have established a central inventory-control point within the Defense Logistics Agency (DLA). However, the different military services require different service levels for common parts. For instance, if the navy requires a 95 % service level, the army may already be satisfied with an 85 % service level for the same part. In this example, component commonality does not lead to different penalty costs, but customer classes are prioritized based on their service requirement.

Yet another military application is given by Nahmias and Demmy (1981): A central supply center provides spare parts for the air bases and faces emergency demands in case of unexpected failures as well as regular replenishment orders. Priority is given to the emergency orders. In this example, the air bases also carry inventory which turns the inventory system into a so-called multi-echelon system, although Nahmias and Demmy (1981) do not analyze it from that perspective. Among others, we will explore the relation of inventory rationing to multi-echelon systems in the next section.

7.2 Related Areas

Closely related to inventory rationing are two other areas in which several demand classes occur in a rather natural way: Multi-echelon systems and revenue management.

In a simple multi-echelon system - visualized in Figure 7.1 - a central warehouse delivers stock to a set of retailers that can be viewed as different customers. The warehouse itself receives replenishment from an outside supplier, but does not necessarily carry inventory at any point of time. In this

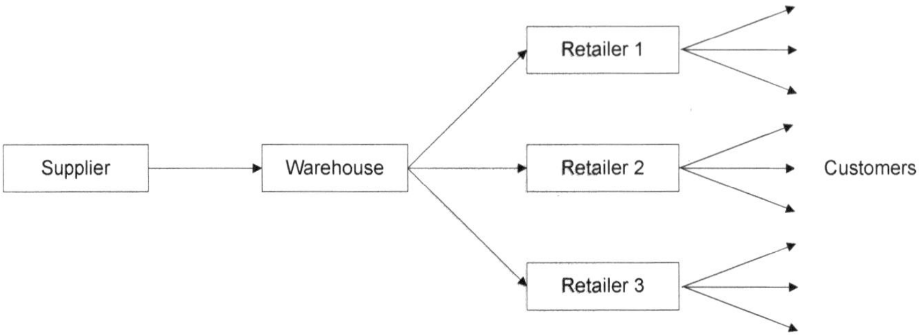

Figure 7.1: A simple divergent multi-echelon system

context, Cohen et al. (1998) outline a system in which a higher echelon, such as the warehouse in Figure 7.1, faces two different kinds of demand from lower echelons, e.g. the retailers in Figure 7.1: Regular replenishment orders and stockout emergency shipments. The latter have priority. If the retailer requires emergency shipments the demand at the retailer is lost. Other systems assume diverse lower echelons. While it might be wise to employ a critical level rationing policy in the situation described by Cohen et al. (1998), the allocation problem in the second situation is not based on different penalty costs or service levels. To sum up, a warehouse with different retailers a priori also faces an allocation decision but the question differs, mainly due to retailers carrying inventories. See Jackson (1988) for an overview of research in this area.

The existence of several customer classes has also long been recognized in the hoteling and airline industries. In these cases, the objective is usually to maximize revenues as the situations are typically characterized by a fixed capacity and a perishable good. Decisions therefore include price and allocation quantity decisions as well as structural decisions concerning the selling process (van Ryzin and Talluri 2005). Purely quantity-based revenue management assumes deterministic prices for the different customer classes. Allocation is commonly controlled by booking limits or protection levels, which bare some resemblance to the critical levels mentioned above (see for instance Belobaba (1989)). However, inventory rationing allows multiple replenishments and capacity is not fixed, but has to be decided upon. While price-based revenue management usually leads to dynamic control policies, inventory rationing is often (but not necessarily) concerned with static control policies as Deshpande et al. (2003) stresses. We refer to van Ryzin and Talluri (2005) for a comprehensive introduction to revenue management and to McGill and van Ryzin (1999) for an overview of the academic research in this area.

7.3 Rationing Rules

If there is more than one customer class, there are two ways to consider this in traditional inventory systems: Either we keep a separate stock for each customer class or we keep one inventory for all and apply a order-up-to level policy based on the demand weighted average penalty costs or the highest required service level. Since it does not take into account the so-called *portfolio effect*, the first method, separate stock for each customer class, does not allow for economies of scale (Eppen and Schrage 1981). We will address the two alternatives again when evaluating our model in Section 9.2 and Section 10.2 respectively.

Alternatively, one might correspond to this situation by keeping one stock and deciding upon arrival of a demand of a certain customer class whether to meet this demand or keep inventory for important future demands. We refer to the policy this decision is based upon as *rationing* or *allocation rule*. A lot of rationing rules have been initially developed for and studied in the multi-echelon context mentioned before.

In an inventory system with multiple customer classes, various intuitive approaches to dividing the inventory among the classes have been analyzed. If penalty costs for the different demand classes are identical, the traditional order-up-to level policy with a FCFS-allocation remains optimal (de Véricourt et al. 2001). If the customer classes differ in their importance for the retailer or manufacturer, the following rationing rules have been studied (among others):

- *Strict Priority Rationing:* While incoming demand is filled on a FCFS basis, backorders are cleared based on priorities immediately after replenishments arrive. For certain parameter constellation this policy can lead to near-optimal result in a capacitated continuous review inventory system (de Véricourt et al. 2001).

- *Proportional Balancing Rule:* Assume a periodic setting. Let d_{it} and b_{it} denote the demand and backorders of customer class i in period t. The customer classes are prioritized based on their penalty costs p_i: The higher the penalty cost the more important the customer class. At the end of period t, the inventory after order arrival i_t is allocated to the customer classes based on their needs, i.e., the sum of backorders from the previous period and current demand, and their importance and each customer class obtains the following share of the available inventory:

$$(d_{it} + b_{it-1}) - \frac{1/p_i}{\sum_j 1/p_j} \max\left\{\sum_j (d_{jt} + b_{jt-1}) - i_t, 0\right\}.$$

  This rationing rule is very efficient if backorder costs are quadratic (Katircioglu and Atkins 1998). A similar balancing policy has been studied by Jackson (1988) in a multi-echelon context.

- *Threshold or Critical Level Rationing:* Under this rationing rule, inventory levels are defined that reserve inventory for customers of more important demand classes. We refer to these rationing levels as *critical* or *rationing levels*[8]. In a system with n demand classes, the rule works as follows: Let the customer classes be ordered by their importance with n denoting the least important customer class. There are $n-1$ rationing levels $CL_i, i = 1, ..., n-1$, with $CL_i \geq 0$ and $CL_i \geq CL_{i-1}$. If the inventory drops to or below the critical level CL_i, then only demand of customer classes $j \leq i$ is met immediately. Demand of less important customer classes is either backordered or lost. Table 7.1 summarizes all cases for a periodic inventory system with two demand classes. As there is only one rationing level, we drop the index and refer to this one as the *critical level* CL.

[8] In the literature, they are also referred to as threshold (rationing) levels.

	Case	Class 1	Class 2	End stock
1	$i_t < d_{1t}$	(p)	(-)	0
2	$i_t \geq d_{1t}$,			
	$i_t - d_{1t} < CL$	(e)	(-)	$i_t - d_{1t}$
3	$i_t - d_{1t} \geq CL$,			
	$i_t - d_{1t} - d_{2t} < CL$	(e)	(p)	CL
4	$i_t - d_{1t} - d_{2t} \geq CL$	(e)	(e)	$i_t - d_{1t} - d_{2t}$

(e) demand filled entirely, (p) demand filled partially, (-) no demand filled

Table 7.1: Critical level rationing for two customer classes

Such a policy has been proven to be optimal for different settings (see Section 7.5.1). As we also study a critical level policy, our further discussion will focus on this rationing rule only.

7.4 Backorders and Backorder Clearing Mechanisms

Tsay et al. (1999) classify the inventory rationing problem in general as a very challenging and analytically and computationally complex problem. In order to optimize a rationing policy, many dimensions have to be taken into account, e.g. the current inventory on hand and the orders in the pipeline (Gayon et al. 2005). In contrast to traditional single-class inventory systems, backorders do not facilitate the analysis of inventory systems with more than one customer class, but enhance complexity significantly.

Periodic review models face the additional difficulty that at the beginning of each period there are both, new demands and backorders. The cost-optimal approach that we refer to as *completely prioritized clearing* clears backorders in the same way as demands are filled. This results in longer waiting times for low priority customers (Dekker et al. 1998), but (under linear penalty costs) minimizes backorder costs as we ensure that incurred backorders are of low priority and thus cheap. In particular, de Véricourt et al. (2001) stress the advantages of this backorder clearing method. As a major drawback of this clearing approach, the inventory level does not incorporate enough information anymore (Nahmias and Demmy 1981). Instead, it is necessary to know the distribution of the stock available at the beginning of each period and the distribution of the backorder level of each class. Positive lead times additionally require tracking orders. These issues are avoided in single period models and facilitated if the lead time is zero (Nahmias and Demmy 1981). For less restrictive settings, some sub-optimal clearing methods have been developed to cope with these difficulties.

The most popular approach clears backorders upon replenishment in the order of their arrivals. The critical level does not influence backorder clearing. We call this approach *immediate backorder clearing.* It has been applied by Arslan et al. (2005) and Tempelmeier (2006).

For two customer classes, another approach has been developed by Deshpande et al. (2003): Inventory exceeding the rationing level is used to clear backorders of both classes under FCFS. The remaining inventory is then used to fill class 1 backorders only. This *threshold clearing* mechanism has been invented in a continuous review (s, Q)-policy, but can easily be applied in a periodic review setting with more than two customer classes.

Some authors, e.g. Topkis (1968) and Nahmias and Demmy (1981) in their continuous review model, also clear backorders prior to serving demand but impose assumptions to exclude the possibility that the inventory after filling backorders drops below the critical level respectively the reorder point.

It is worth noting that continuous review policies do not encounter the problem of concurrent new demand and backorders. Furthermore, under $(S-1, S)$-replenishment with demands following Poisson processes, replenishments consist of one unit only and backorder clearing follows directly from the critical level policy. For this reason, results valid in the continuous review context may not be transferred easily to periodic review settings. However, especially in systems operating under (s, Q)-replenishments, it might happen that clearing backorders upon replenishment arrival yields an inventory below the rationing level.

7.5 Literature Review

Literature on critical level rationing has addressed various research objectives in diverse settings. There are articles trying to characterize the optimal inventory rationing policy in a specific setting. Others assume that a certain policy is in place and analyze the results. The settings considered range from continuous review to periodic review models, considering Poisson demands only or allowing arbitrary stochastic demands, assuming different replenishment policies and various possibilities for the lead time. If unmet demand is backordered, various clearing mechanisms have been studied (see Section 7.4).

To structure this manifold of literature, the review is divided into three parts: Section 7.5.1 presents those articles trying to characterize the optimal policy for a certain situation. Section 7.5.2 covers those papers evaluating and optimizing a given policy. Finally, Section 7.5.3 deals with critical level rationing being studied in other context.

7.5.1 Characterizations of the Optimal Policy

The articles in this first section of the literature review focus on the following question: What is the general structure of the optimal policy for a specific setting? Although the whole field of inventory rationing started with this question, this question is less-researched than the effects of a given policy. After Evans (1968), Kaplan (1968), Topkis (1968) and Veinott (1965b) published their results in the late 1960s, nothing has been done until 1997 when Ha (1997a, 1997b) presented a completely new approach to the problem.

In this section, we will review this work divided into periodic and continuous review models. Commonly, the models in this area assume penalty costs or lost revenues as means to distinguish between different customer groups instead of service levels.

Periodic Review Models

A special kind of critical level rationing was first suggested by Veinott (1965b). In his periodic inventory system with n customer classes all critical levels equal zero. Most of his other assumptions concerning the cost structure and demand distributions are rather general and under certain conditions he is able to show that this critical level rationing policy is optimal.

Independently, Evans (1968), Kaplan (1968) and Topkis (1968) showed a couple of years later that critical level rationing with non-zero rationing levels is also optimal in more general settings. The last author is often referred to as the founder of critical level rationing because his results were the most general among those three. In contrast to Evans (1968) and Kaplan (1968), Topkis (1968) allowed not only two but an arbitrary number of customer classes. In detail, he studied the following model:

- Replenishment is assumed to occur periodically.
- Each replenishment interval is subdivided into shorter periods in which demands are observed.
- Demand may be either backlogged, partially backordered or completely lost.
- Demand that is backlogged at the end of one interval may be satisfied at the end of a later interval within the same replenishment cycle.
- Once the stock is replenished, all backlogged demand has to be satisfied first (immediate backorder clearing).
- Ordering, holding and (if applicable) penalty costs are required to be linear.

The resulting optimal policy has time-dependent threshold structure. While Topkis (1968) in general assumes instantaneous order arrivals, he provides conditions under which the rationing policy is myopic.

After Topkis (1968) only Frank et al. (2003) also address the question of the optimal policy in a periodic setting. They analyze a periodic review inventory system with two demand classes and one period lead time. The demand of the higher prioritized class is deterministic and the demand of the lower prioritized class is stochastic. Each period, the deterministic demand has to be met (100 % service level requirement). Stochastic demand might be rationed in which case it is lost. In addition to the costs considered by the four pioneers, Frank et al. (2003) include setup cost in their considerations. For this system, they partially characterize the structure of the optimal policy and show that the optimal order quantity and rationing policy are state-dependent and do not have a simple structure. They develop a heuristic and show that it performs well in a variety of settings.

Ha and the Continuous Review Models

Thirty years after the four pioneering articles have been published, Ha (1997a) proves the optimality of a critical level policy in an infinite horizon $M/M/1/S$ queuing model for an inventory system with one stock serving n demand classes. Demand rates follow Poisson processes and unmet demand is lost. The stock itself is replenished endogenously with exponentially distributed lead time and production capacity is limited. Table 7.2 shows how Ha interprets the events and statistics known from queueing theory.

Queueing Theory	Ha's Interpretation
waiting customers	current inventory
customer arrival	newly produced item
service completion	filled demand
limit of waiting room	capacity of production facility

Table 7.2: Relations between queueing theory and Ha's model

Ha (1997a) considers holding cost and lost revenues. The optimal replenishment policy then turns out to be of *lot-for-lot kind.* Due to the continuous supply, the model is memoryless. Thus the critical levels are time-independent. For two demand classes, Ha (1997b) also characterizes the optimal policy for the backorder case. The critical levels are now decreasing in the backorder levels of the lower priority class. This work has been extended to n demand classes by de Véricourt et al. (2002) who also provides an algorithm to actually determine the optimal rationing levels.

In his later paper, Ha (2000) modifies his lost sales model to Erlang-distributed lead times. Partially completed production is taken into account and the critical levels are revised accordingly. The corresponding model including backorders has been studied by Gayon et al. (2005).

7.5.2 Evaluations and Optimizations of Critical Level Policies

A second stream of research assumes that for a certain setting a specific rationing policy is in place. Two objectives are commonly pursued: Deepening the understanding of the effects of a rationing policy and optimizing a given critical level policy. Articles in the first group evaluate the benefits of the policy, such as fill rate development or benefits of heuristic approaches. The second group focusses on optimizing the parameters of the policy, e.g. determining the optimal order-up-to level.

In this research area, customer differentiation is not always taken into account based on penalty or shortage costs but is also achieved requiring different service levels. Thus base stock and critical levels are supposed to simply minimize costs or to additionally comply with certain service requirements.

We now provide an overview on the articles exclusively studying the effects of rationing on an inventory system before running through those minimizing the cost objective and those focusing on the service-constraint inventory rationing problem.

Analyses of Rationing Policies

The first authors who systematically analyze a threshold rationing policy are Nahmias and Demmy (1981). Assuming a constant rationing level, they derive expressions for the fill rates in a periodic inventory system with two customer classes and zero lead time. Unfulfilled demand is backordered and cleared after order arrival at the beginning of the next period. They show that the ratio of total backorders in this rationing system and backorders in a FCFS-environment increases in the constant critical level, i.e., the total amount of backorders increases in the critical level. However, the fill rate for high priority customers improves significantly. These results are extended to n customer classes by Moon and Kang (1998). To allow for a positive lead time, Nahmias and Demmy (1981) also introduce the first continuous review inventory rationing model. They again assume two classes, a constant critical level and backorders that are cleared as in the periodic setting. The two demands are now assumed to follow Poisson processes. Replenishment is governed by an (s, Q)-policy with at most one outstanding order. This restriction allows the authors to identify the net inventory with the inventory position. Conditioning on the *hitting time*, i.e., the time the net inventory hits the rationing level, Nahmias and Demmy (1981) derive results similar to those for their periodic model.

Assuming $(S-1, S)$-replenishment, Dekker et al. (1998) are able to drop the assumption of at most one outstanding order of Nahmias and Demmy (1981). However, they do not study a strict critical level policy. Even if upon replenishment the inventory is below the critical level, a low priority backorder is cleared if the replenishment was originally triggered by a low priority demand. This way they combine a high service level for high priority customers with reduced waiting times for low priority customers. They also employ the hitting time approach to derive approximations for the fill rates. By means of simulation, they compare these to the "real" fill rates achieved assuming three different clearing mechanisms. For the same setting but with strict critical level policy, Fadiloglu and Bulut (2005) present a method to determine the exact steady state probabilities for the backorders (and thus the fill rates) based on Markov chain theory.

de Véricourt et al. (2001) compare their optimal critical level policy (de Véricourt et al. 2002) with the strict priority policy outlined in Section 7.3 and the traditional FCFS policy. The setting is the same as detailed for Ha (1997b) in the preceding section. They show that the critical level outperforms the other two policies in terms of average cost, although under certain conditions the two benchmark policies may achieve results very close or even identical to the optimal policy.

Finally, Tempelmeier (2006) focuses on performance measures such as the waiting time for class 2 customers in a periodic review system with two customer classes with backordering managed by a (s, Q, CL)-policy. While demands in his model are arbitrarily distributed, lead time is deterministic and backorders are completely cleared in an unprioritized way at the beginning of each period.

Cost Minimization

For the reasons already mentioned before, lost sales models have enjoyed far more attention when it comes to finding the optimal parameters for a given rationing policy.

Melchiors et al. (2000) essentially optimize the model of Nahmias and Demmy (1981) assuming lost sales instead of backordering. They derive an expression for the average expected cost per time unit including shortage, inventory holding and order setup costs. The numerical optimization procedure is based on enumeration and bounding. Assuming a stochastic lead time, Dekker et al. (2002) are able to derive exact formulae for the backorder probabilities for each of n customer classes in a $(S-1, S)$-inventory system. They provide a numerical solution algorithm and a heuristic solution approach and present some structural results. The numerical solution algorithm has been improved most recently by Kranenburg and van Houtum (2006a) who develop three very efficient heuristics that all find the optimal solution.

Also in a lost sales environment, Melchiors (2003) studies a system with non-static rationing levels and provides a numerical study to underline the superiority of his policy over the constant rationing policy. He assumes a continuous review (s, Q)-policy, n customer classes with demands following Poisson processes, a deterministic lead time and at most one outstanding order. Similar to Topkis (1968), the lead time is divided into subintervals and the critical levels decrease with the number of remaining subintervals until the next replenishment. During each subinterval the rationing levels are constant. Empirical observations enable Melchiors (2003) to provide a numerical algorithm for finding the optimal parameters of his policy in each subinterval.

The heuristic approach of Frank et al. (2003) assuming a constant critical level also has to be mentioned here (see Section 7.5.1 for details of their model).

Assuming backordering, Deshpande et al. (2003) optimize the base stock and rationing levels for a continuous review (s, Q)-policy with two customer classes and arbitrary stochastic demand. To derive an expression for the average cost, they have to assume the alternative clearing mechanism outlined in Section 7.4: Inventory exceeding the rationing level is used to clear backorders of both classes under FCFS. The remaining inventory is then used to fill class 1 backorders only. They show that their policy is superior to traditional approaches.

The recent work of Enders et al. (2006) finally considers a mixed lost-sales and backordering problem. They study a continuous review system with $(S-1, S)$-replenishment and exponentially distributed lead time. Demands of the two customer classes follow Poisson processes. While unfilled demand of the high priority class is lost, low priority demand is backordered. This system is numerically optimized based on Markov chain theory.

Service-Level Constrained Rationing

Work on service-constrained models mainly assumes a continuous setting and thus Poisson demands. Although all the lost sales models described in the preceding section implicitly derive exact or approximate expression for the fill rates, the authors mainly restrict themselves to the pure cost minimization problem. As an exception, Dekker et al. (2002) provide solution algorithms for the service-constraint inventory rationing problem based on their exact fill rate expressions in the lost sales continuous review model described in Section 7.5.2.

Recently, Arslan et al. (2005) numerically determine the steady state distribution of the inventory level in a continuous review system with multiple demand classes, deterministic lead time and backordering. Their approach is based on a 1-1-mapping of a serial n-stage system and a system with n customer classes and involves non-optimal immediate backorder clearing. Based on the inventory levels they provide an approximative solution algorithm for the service-constraint rationing problem and give an upper bound for the gap between this approximation and their original model.

Periodic review models applying service constraints are only studied by Katircioglu and Atkins (1998), Cohen et al. (1998) and Tempelmeier (2006). Katircioglu and Atkins (1998) present a myopic solution for a service constraint rationing problem with two customer classes. Relaxing some inventory constraints, this solution optimizes the allocation quantities under quadratic penalty costs and does not explicitly include the idea of a critical level (see also Section 7.3). Cohen et al. (1998) who assume a critical level of zero (although they do not explicitly say this), include setup costs as well as inventory holding and delivery costs. However, their objective is different because they search for the order-up-to level minimizing the average cost subject to a system fill rate constraint. Eventually, Tempelmeier (2006) provides some fill rate approximations for a system with two customer classes managed by a (R, s, S, CL)-policy which he then applies to optimize the three parameters. However, as already mentioned he mainly focuses on performance measures such as the waiting time for class 2 customers and applies immediate backorder clearing.

7.5.3 Other Studies Involving Critical Level Rationing

Only most recently, critical level rationing has been considered in other than single-item, single-location inventory systems. Aspects other than lead time, costs or service levels have been taken into account that might influence the policy.

Critical level rationing has been shown to be optimal in systems with (imperfect) information about future demands (Gayon et al. 2004). The modeling framework coincides with that of Ha (1997a). Interestingly, the higher the amount of announced orders of a customer class the higher the resulting optimal rationing level for this class. The authors show that advanced demand information (ADI) leads to cost reductions complementary to those incurred by inventory rationing without ADI.

Based on the models of Ha (1997a) and Dekker et al. (1998), Äxsater et al. (2004) provide the only study of critical level policies in a multi-echelon system. They consider a one warehouse, n retailer inventory system with Poisson demands at each retailer and the warehouse. Unmet demand occurring at a retailer is backlogged whereas it is lost when occurring at the warehouse. If the warehouse does not deliver to the retailers, emergency shipments are placed at outside suppliers. The costs the retailers face for those emergency shipments form the basis for critical level policy the warehouse applies. In this setting, the authors define a heuristic algorithm to optimize the critical levels and order-up-to levels for each retailer and present bounds for the total cost of the system.

Most recently, Kranenburg and van Houtum (2006b) study the benefits of critical level rationing in a multi-item spare parts inventory system. For each customer group, i.e., a set of machines, each spare part is controlled at the central warehouse by a continuous-review critical level policy. Demands of each customer group for each spare part follow a constant Poisson process. If the warehouse decides not to fulfill the request for a spare part by a certain customer group, the demand is filled by an emergency shipment from an outside supplier and thus lost for the warehouse. Lead times are stochastic and depend on the kind of shipment as well as the spare part. The system is optimized regarding the overall average spare parts provisioning costs subject to some waiting time constraints for the different customer groups. Those costs are calculated based on costs for regular replenishments and costs for emergency shipments.

7.6 Classification of Our Work

Our work is concerned with periodic inventory rationing in the presence of (deterministic) lead time under completely prioritized backorder clearing. We consider two customer classes with arbitrary stochastic demand. For the major part of the remaining thesis, the inventory system is controlled by a (R, S)-policy with a constant rationing level CL.

Figure 7.2 gives a classification of our research on constant critical level rationing. It lists all research concerned with critical level policies for lead times greater than zero and one. For the ease of presentation, we incude both, pure cost minimizatin and service-constraint minimization (the latter indicated by *). We subsummize all work either assuming a non-optimal backorder clearing mechanism or applying approximations in their analysis as "approximate".

	CONTINUOUS REVIEW (S-1,S)		CONTINUOUS REVIEW (s,Q)		PERIODIC REVIEW	
	Backorders	Lost Sales	Backorders	Lost Sales	Backorders	Lost Sales
EXACT	Ha (1997b), de Véricourt et al. (2002), Gayon et al. (2005)	Ha (1997a), Ha (2000), Dekker et al. (2002)*		Melchiors et al. (2000)	OUR WORK	
APPROXIMATE	Dekker et al. (1998)*	Dekker et al. (2002)*, Kranenbourg and van Houtum (2006)	Nahmias and Demmy (1981), Deshpande et al. (2003), Arslan et al. (2005)*	Melchiors (2003)	Tempelmeier (2006)*	Cohen et al. (1988)*

Figure 7.2: Research on critical level policies with positive lead time

We have already outlined that results for continuous review inventory systems cannot be easily translated to periodic review settings. Thus our work contributes to the research in a significant way. Additionally, our assumption, in particular concerning the demand distribution, are more general and we not only optimize our policy but also provide insight into the steady state behavior as such.

The study on dynamic rationing levels resembles in its structure the work of de Véricourt et al. (2001) although the modeling assumptions are entirely different. As orders arrive each period, the dynamics of our rationing level do not depend on the time until the next replenishment, as Melchiors (2003) suggests, but on the amount of orders in the pipeline.

Chapter 8

A Markov-Chain Based Modeling Approach

In this chapter, we introduce our core model. We explain the sequence of events, derive the fundamental role of class 2 backorders and introduce our approach to model those.

Note that we are using an inventory policy with a static critical level where rationing decision are based on the on-hand inventory level. In most situations, this policy will not be optimal, because a critical level and a rationing decision that depend on the entire state of the inventory system, i.e., on the open orders of individual previous periods and the backorder/inventory levels, would result in lower expected cost. However, finding the optimal policy is likely to be analytically intractable (for a discussion of this issue see Deshpande et al. (2003), Frank et al. (2003), Kleijn and Dekker (1998), Topkis (1968)) and the optimal policy is most likely difficult to implement. The static critical level policy we analyze can be solved optimally and is easy to implement.

We next present our model (Section 8.1). We derive recursive equations for the backorder levels and this way establish the fundamental role of class 2 backorders (Section 8.2). In Section 8.3, we then introduce the underlying Markov chain. Finally, we present some structural results (Section 8.4). All

K. Möllering, *Inventory Rationing*, Edition KWV,
https://doi.org/10.1007/978-3-658-24255-8_8

proofs are contained in Section 8.5.

8.1 Modeling Framework

We consider a periodic review inventory system with two customer classes. We denote class 1 demand in period t by D_{1t} and class 2 demand in period t by D_{2t}. D_{1t} and D_{2t} are each i.i.d. discrete random variables and can be arbitrarily distributed. Replenishment orders arrive after a lead time of LT periods. Demand that is not filled during a period is backordered.

Inventory is controlled by a threshold inventory rationing policy with a constant critical level CL. The sequence of events in each period is as follows. At the beginning of period t, we receive the order that was placed $LT+1$ periods before and determine the on-hand inventory level I_t. Then, we observe the demands D_{1t} and D_{2t} of the current period. We fill class 1 backorders from previous periods and class 1 demand of the current period. If the remaining on-hand inventory is above the critical level CL, we fill class 2 backorders from previous periods and class 2 demand of the current period until all backorders and demands have been filled or the on-hand inventory reaches CL. Next, we determine the on-hand inventory level at the end of the period IH_t, the backorder levels for class 1 and 2 customers B_{1t} and B_{2t}, and determine the total cost of period t according to our objective. Finally, we place a replenishment order such that the inventory position (on-hand inventory minus backorders plus open orders) is S. Since S is static, we reorder at the end of each period t the total demand of that period, $D_t = D_{1t} + D_{2t}$. This order arrives at the beginning of period $t + LT + 1$. The amount of inventory on order at the beginning of period t after order arrival is referred to as $IO_t = D_{t-1} + ... + D_{t-LT}$.

8.2 Recursive Expressions for Backorders

The critical level policy allocates inventory based on the on-hand inventory at the beginning of a period I_t, the backorder levels at the end of the previous period B_{1t-1} and B_{2t-1}, and the demands of the period D_{1t} and D_{2t}. The on-hand inventory I_t at the beginning of a period is first used to fill class 1 backorders of the previous previous period B_{1t-1} and class 1 demands of the current period D_{1t}. If $I_t \geq B_{1t-1} + D_{1t}$, then all class 1 backorders are cleared and all class 1 demands are filled. If $I_t < B_{1t-1} + D_{1t}$, some class 1 demand is backordered. So, the backorder level of class 1 can be computed as

$$B_{1t} = [B_{1t-1} + D_{1t} - I_t]^+ . \tag{8.1}$$

The computation of the backorder level of class 2 demand is more complex. If the on-hand inventory after filling all class 1 backorders and demand is greater than the critical level CL, i.e., if $I_t - B_{1t-1} - D_{1t} > CL$, then some or all class 2 backorders and demands are filled and the resulting class 2 backorder level is $B_{2t} = [B_{2t-1} + D_{2t} - I_t + B_{1t-1} + D_{1t} + CL]^+$. If the on-hand inventory after filling all class 1 backorders and demand is less than or equal to the critical level CL, i.e., if $I_t - B_{1t-1} - D_{1t} \leq CL$, then no inventory is available for clearing class 2 backorders or filling class 2 demand and the resulting class 2 backorder level is $B_{2t} = B_{2t-1} + D_{2t}$. So,

$$B_{2t} = \begin{cases} [B_{2t-1} + D_{2t} - I_t + B_{1t-1} + D_{1t} + CL]^+ & \text{if } (I) > CL \\ B_{2t-1} + D_{2t} & \text{if } (I) \leq CL, \end{cases} \tag{8.2}$$

where (I) stands for $I_t - B_{1t-1} - D_{1t}$. Backorder levels of class 1 and class 2 depend on the on-hand inventory at the beginning of the period, I_t. I_t can be computed as

$$I_t = S - IO_t + B_{1t-1} + B_{2t-1}. \tag{8.3}$$

We charge inventory holding cost against the inventory at the end of a period. Since the order quantity that is received at the beginning of period $t+1$ is equal to the demand of Period $t - LT$, the ending inventory of period t is

$$IH_t = I_{t+1} - D_{t-LT}. \tag{8.4}$$

We next simplify the expressions for class 1 and 2 backorders by substituting I_t in Equations (8.1) and (8.2) by the expression from Equation (8.3):

$$B_{1t} = [D_{1t} - S + IO_t - B_{2t-1}]^+ , \tag{8.5}$$

and

$$B_{2t} = \begin{cases} [D_{1t} + D_{2t} - S + IO_t + CL]^+ & \text{if } S - IO_t + B_{2t-1} - D_{1t} > CL \\ B_{2t-1} + D_{2t} & \text{if } S - IO_t + B_{2t-1} - D_{1t} \leq CL. \end{cases} \tag{8.6}$$

Note that we now express B_{2t} in Equation (8.6) in terms of B_{2t-1} and previous demands, but that B_{2t} no longer depends on B_{1t}. This implies that we can compute the distribution of B_{2t} and its expectation independently of B_{1t}. Also note that we can express B_{1t} in Equation (8.5) in terms of B_{2t-1} and previous demand, which implies that we can compute the distribution of B_{1t} and its expectation easily once we know the distribution of B_{2t}. After we have computed the expectations of B_{1t} and B_{2t}, we can compute the expected inventory at the end of a period by Equations (8.3) and (8.4) which completes the computation of all components of our cost function. So, if we know the distribution of B_{2t}, everything else follows. Next, we show how the inventory system can be modeled using a Markov chain and provide some structural results for both classes of backorders and the expected inventory at the end of a period.

8.3 Markov Chain

Class 2 backorders in period t depend on the class 2 backorder level in period $t-1$ and on the demands of periods $t-LT$ to $t-1$. Given b_{2t-1} and $d_{t-1}, d_{t-2}, \ldots, d_{t-LT}$, we can be compute b_{2t} using Equation (8.6). We thus use the state space

$$x_t = (b_{2t-1}, d_{t-1}, d_{t-2}, \ldots, d_{t-LT}).$$

The states x_t form a discrete Markov chain and we are interested in the stationary behavior of the Markov chain. Proposition 11 states that the Markov chain has a unique stationary distribution. The proofs of this and all other propositions in this chapter are contained in Section 8.5.

Proposition 11 *For any discrete i.i.d. distributions with* $\Pr(D_{1t} = d_{1t}) > 0$ *and* $\Pr(D_{2t} = d_{2t}) > 0$ *for all* $d_{it}, i = 1, 2,$ *the Markov chain is irreducible,* *aperiodic, and positive recurrent and therefore has a unique stationary distribution.*

Note that in case of demand distributions with a maximum possible demand the Markov chain only admits one finite closed class and is still aperiodic. Thus for the reduced state space, we still obtain a unique limit distribution.

Once we have computed the distribution of the steady states x, it is straightforward to extract the distribution of class 2 backorders. Furthermore, we may compute the distribution of class 1 backorders from the distribution of the steady states x. All these information together finally allows us to also derive the expected inventory on hand at the end of a period.

Next, we provide some structural results for the backorder levels and the cost function.

8.4 Structural Results

We now analyze how the distributions and the expectations of backorders and inventory levels depend on the order-up-to level S and the critical level CL. These results are interesting in their own rights and they form the basis for the optimization of both, the penalty cost model in Chapter 9 as well as the service constraint model in Chapter 10.

Let $F_{B_2}^{S,CL}(b_2)$ denote the c.d.f. of class 2 backorders for an inventory system with order-up-to level S and critical level CL. Proposition 12 states that $F_{B_2}^{S+1,CL}(b_2) \geq F_{B_2}^{S,CL}(b_2)$ and that $F_{B_2}^{S,CL+1}(b_2) \leq F_{B_2}^{S,CL}(b_2)$, i.e., that class 2 backorders are stochastically decreasing in S and stochastically increasing in CL. We use the terms increasing and decreasing non-strictly to refer to non-decreasing and non-increasing functions.

Proposition 12 *Class 2 backorders are stochastically decreasing in S, i.e.,*

$$F_{B_2}^{S+1,CL}(b_2) \geq F_{B_2}^{S,CL}(b_2)$$

and stochastically increasing in CL, i.e.,

$$F_{B_2}^{S,CL+1}(b_2) \leq F_{B_2}^{S,CL}(b_2).$$

The results of Proposition 12 are intuitive. If we increase the order-up-to level S and keep the critical level CL constant, we have more units available for filling class 2 demand. Therefore, the probability of having b_2 or fewer backorders is higher with a order-up-to level of $S+1$ than with a order-up-to level of S. If we increase the critical level from CL to $CL+1$, we reserve more inventory for class 1 demand and have less inventory available for class 2 demand. Therefore, the probability of having b_2 or fewer backorders is lower with a critical level of $CL+1$ than with a critical level of CL. Proposition 13 states similar results for class 1 backorders, where $F_{B_1}^{S,CL}(b_1)$ denotes the c.d.f. of class 1 backorders.

Proposition 13 *Class 1 backorders are stochastically decreasing in S, i.e.,*

$$F_{B_1}^{S+1,CL}(b_1) \geq F_{B_1}^{S,CL}(b_1)$$

and stochastically decreasing in CL, i.e.,

$$F_{B_1}^{S,CL+1}(b_1) \geq F_{B_1}^{S,CL}(b_1).$$

The effect of changes in S and CL on the inventory at the end of a period is stated in Proposition 14, where $F_{IH}^{S,CL}(ih)$ denotes the c.d.f. of the on-hand inventory level at the end of a period.

Proposition 14 *The on-hand inventory level at the end of a period is stochastically increasing in S, i.e.,*

$$F_{IH}^{S+1,CL}(ih) \leq F_{IH}^{S,CL}(ih)$$

and stochastically increasing in CL, i.e.,

$$F_{IH}^{S,CL+1}(ih) \leq F_{IH}^{S,CL}(ih).$$

As we would expect, decreasing the order-up-to level S or the critical level CL leads to a higher probability of having low inventory levels.

Applying Proposition 7, the results of Propositions 12 to 14 lead immediately to Corollary 2 that states the effect of changes in the order-up-to level S and critical level CL on expected backorder and inventory levels.

Corollary 2 *The following properties hold for the backorder and inventory levels:*

a. *The expected amount of class 2 backorders is decreasing in S and increasing in CL, i.e., $EB_2^{S+1,CL} \leq EB_2^{S,CL}$ and $EB_2^{S,CL+1} \geq EB_2^{S,CL}$.*

b. *The expected amount of class 1 backorders is decreasing in S and CL, i.e., $EB_1^{S+1,CL} \leq EB_1^{S,CL}$ and $EB_1^{S,CL+1} \leq EB_1^{S,CL}$.*

c. *The expected on-hand inventory at the end of a period is increasing in S and CL, i.e., $EIH^{S+1,CL} \geq EIH^{S,CL}$ and $EIH^{S,CL+1} \geq EIH^{S,CL}$.*

For Poisson demands with $\lambda_1 = 1.50$, $\lambda_2 = 0.75$, lead time $LT = 2$ and critical level $CL = 0$, the effect of changes in the order-up-to level S on expected backorder and inventory levels is shown in Figure 8.1. For $S = 5$, the effect of changes in the critical level CL on expected backorder and inventory levels is shown in Figure 8.2.

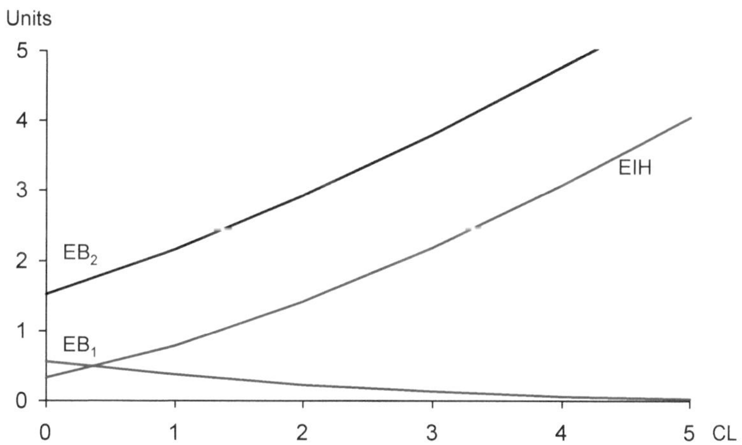

Figure 8.1: Effect of S on EB_1, EB_2 and EIH for given CL

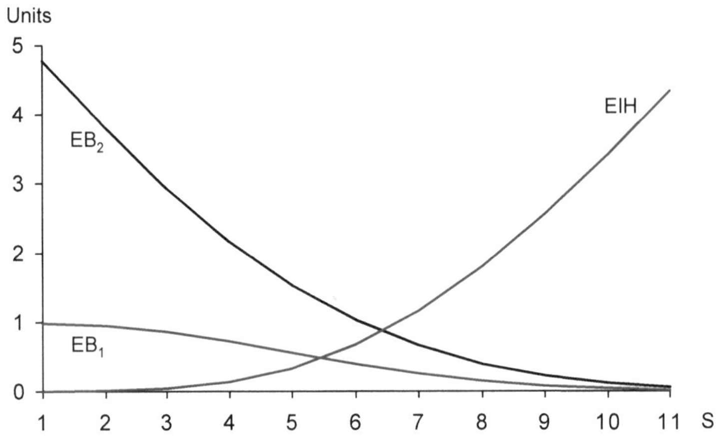

Figure 8.2: Effect of CL on EB_1, EB_2, and EIH for given S

8.5 Proofs

Proof of Proposition 11.

1. The Markov chain is irreducible.

   By Definition 5, a Markov chain is called irreducible if all states communicate. Communication is a transitive property (see Section 4.4). If two states i and j communicate and so do j and a third state k, then i and k communicate. Thus to prove communication for all states of the $(LT+1)$-dimensional Markov chain it suffices to prove that there is one state with which all other states communicate. We will show that state $z = (0, 0, ..., 0)$ can be reached from any state and that all states can be reached from state z.

   Let the system be in an arbitrary state y. There is a positive probability that the demand of both classes is zero for $LT + 1$ periods. After such a demand realization, we have zero class 2 backorders. So, any state y communicates with the state $z = (0, 0, ..., 0)$.

   We next show that an arbitrary state $y = (b_{2t-1}, d_{t-1}, \ldots, d_{t-LT})$ can be reached from z. Assume that in period $t - LT - 2$ the system is in state $z = (0, 0, ..., 0)$ and demand in the next period is $d_{t-LT-1} =$

$d_{1t-LT-1} + d_{2t-LT-1}$ with $d_{1t-LT-1} \geq S - CL$ and $d_{2t-LT-1} = b_{2t-1}$. Then class 2 demand will be completely backordered in this period. There is a positive probability that demand in periods $t - LT$ to $t - 1$ is completely caused by class 1 customers, i.e., $d_{t-i} = d_{1t-i}$ for $i = 1, ..., LT$. Then, no additional class 2 backorders will be incurred but due to the level of outstanding orders existing class 2 backorders will not be cleared either. Thus in period t the system is in state $y = (b_{2t-1}, d_{t-1}, \ldots, d_{t-LT})$. This proves that z communicates with any state y.

2. The Markov chain is aperiodic.
   By Proposition 1, aperiodicity is a class property, i.e., if one state of the class fulfills this property, so do all other states. Thus it again suffices to show aperiodicity for one state only.
   Let the Markov chain be in state $z = (0, 0, ..., 0)$. A sufficient criterion for aperiodicity of z is the existence of a self-loop, i.e. there is a positive probability p_{zz} to return to z in one step. Now $p_{zz} = \Pr(D_t = 0) > 0$. Thus the state z and hence the Markov chain are aperiodic.

3. The Markov chain is positive recurrent.
   By Proposition 2, positive recurrency is also a class property. Thus it suffices to prove positive recurrency for one state. We will again focus on $z = (0, 0, ..., 0)$.
   It suffices to prove that the steady state probability $\Pr(z)$ of z is greater than zero (Theorem 1). Proving irreducibility, we showed that z is reached whenever $D_t = ... = D_{t-LT} = 0$. Thus $\Pr(z) \geq \Pr(D_t = ... = D_{t-LT} = 0)$. By assumption, this is greater than zero.

□

Proof of Proposition 12.

To prove that class 2 backorders are stochastically decreasing in S, we analyze the sample paths of class 2 backorders with order-up-to levels $S+1$ and S. Although it would be sufficient to prove $b_{2t}^{S+1,CL} \leq b_{2t}^{S,CL}$ for all $t \geq 0$ we will prove by induction over t that $b_{2t}^{S,CL} - b_{2t}^{S+1,CL} \in \{0, 1\}$ for all $t \geq 0$.

Base case: We start in period $t = 1$. Demands in previous periods are zero. Obviously, $b_{20}^{S+1,CL} = b_{20}^{S,CL} = 0$. To analyze class 2 backorders in period 1, we analyze Equation (8.6) for arbitrary demand realizations d_{11} and d_{21} ($io_1 = 0$). Under our initial conditions, Equation (8.6) can be written as

$$b_{21}^{S,CL} = \begin{cases} [d_{11} + d_{21} - S + CL]^+ & \text{if } S - d_{11} > CL \quad \text{(A)} \\ d_{21} & \text{if } S - d_{11} \leq CL \quad \text{(B).} \end{cases} \tag{8.7}$$

and one of the following three cases holds:

Case 1: $b_{21}^{S+1,CL}$ and $b_{21}^{S,CL}$ are computed by part (A) of Equation (8.7). Then, $b_{21}^{S,CL} - b_{21}^{S+1,CL} = [d_{11} + d_{21} - S + CL]^+ - [d_{11} + d_{21} - S - 1 + CL]^+$. Thus either $b_{21}^{S,CL} = b_{21}^{S+1,CL} = 0$ or $b_{21}^{S,CL} - b_{21}^{S+1,CL} = 1$.

Case 2: $b_{21}^{S+1,CL}$ is computed by part (A) and $b_{21}^{S,CL}$ is computed by part (B) of Equation (8.7). The conditions $S + 1 - d_{11} > CL$ and $S - d_{11} \leq CL$ imply that $S - d_{11} = CL$. So, $b_{21}^{S,CL} - b_{21}^{S+1,CL} = d_{21} - [d_{11} + d_{21} - S - 1 + CL]^+$ $= d_{21} - [d_{21} - 1]^+$. Thus either $d_{21} = 0$ and hence $b_{21}^{S,CL} = b_{21}^{S+1,CL} = 0$ or $b_{21}^{S,CL} - b_{21}^{S+1,CL} = 1$.

Case 3: $b_{21}^{S+1,CL}$ and $b_{21}^{S,CL}$ are computed by part (B) of Equation (8.7). Then, $b_{21}^{S,CL} - b_{21}^{S+1,CL} = d_{21} - d_{21} = 0$.

In all three cases we have either $b_{21}^{S+1,CL} = b_{21}^{S,CL}$ or $b_{21}^{S,CL} - b_{21}^{S+1,CL} = 1$ and therefore $b_{21}^{S,CL} - b_{21}^{S+1,CL} \in \{0, 1\}$ holds in general.

Induction hypothesis: Assume that in period $t - 1$ class 2 backorders with order-up-to level S and class 2 backorders with order-up-to level $S + 1$ differ by 1 at most, i.e., $b_{2t-1}^{S,CL} - b_{2t-1}^{S+1,CL} \in \{0, 1\}$.

Induction step: To prove that $b_{2t}^{S,CL} - b_{2t}^{S+1,CL} \in \{0, 1\}$, we analyze Equation (8.6) for arbitrary demand realizations d_{1t}, d_{2t}, and io_t:

$$b_{2t}^{S,CL} = \begin{cases} [d_{1t} + d_{2t} - S + io_t + CL]^+ & \text{if } S - io_t + b_{2t-1}^{S,CL} - d_{1t} > CL \quad \text{(A)} \\ b_{2t-1}^{S,CL} + d_{2t} & \text{if } S - io_t + b_{2t-1}^{S,CL} - d_{1t} \leq CL \quad \text{(B).} \end{cases} \tag{8.8}$$

and analyze the following three cases:

Case 1: $b_{2t}^{S+1,CL}$ and $b_{2t}^{S,CL}$ are computed by part (A) of Equation (8.8). So, $b_{2t}^{S,CL} - b_{2t}^{S+1,CL} = [d_{1t} + d_{2t} - S + io_t + CL]^+ - [d_{1t} + d_{2t} - S - 1 + io_t + CL]^+$. Thus either $b_{2t}^{S,CL} = b_{2t}^{S+1,CL} = 0$ or $b_{2t}^{S,CL} - b_{2t}^{S+1,CL} = 1$.

Case 2: $b_{2t}^{S+1,CL}$ is computed by part (A) and $b_{2t}^{S,CL}$ is computed by part (B) of Equation (8.8). The condition of part (A) may be re-written as $d_{1t} - S - 1 + io_t + CL < b_{2t-1}^{S+1,CL}$, the condition of part (B) as $d_{1t} - S + io_t + CL \geq b_{2t-1}^{S,CL}$. By induction hypothesis, this case can thus only occur if $b_{2t-1}^{S,CL} = b_{2t-1}^{S+1,CL}$ and $d_{1t} - S + io_t + CL = b_{2t-1}^{S,CL}$. So, $b_{2t}^{S,CL} - b_{2t}^{S+1,CL} = b_{2t-1}^{S,CL} + d_{2t} - [d_{1t} + d_{2t} - S - 1 + io_t + CL]^+ = b_{2t-1}^{S,CL} + d_{2t} - [b_{2t-1}^{S,CL} + d_{2t} - 1]^+$ and $b_{2t}^{S,CL} - b_{2t}^{S+1,CL} = 1$ or $b_{2t}^{S,CL} - b_{2t}^{S+1,CL} = 0$.

Case 3: $b_{2t}^{S+1,CL}$ and $b_{2t}^{S,CL}$ are computed by part (B) of Equation (8.8). Because of $b_{2t}^{S,CL} - b_{2t}^{S+1,CL} = b_{2t-1}^{S,CL} + d_{2t} - b_{2t-1}^{S+1,CL} - d_{2t} = b_{2t-1}^{S,CL} - b_{2t-1}^{S+1,CL}$, $b_{2t}^{S,CL} - b_{2t}^{S+1,CL} \in \{0,1\}$ by induction hypothesis.

In all three cases we have $b_{2t}^{S,CL} - b_{2t}^{S+1,CL} \in \{0,1\}$ and therefore $b_{2t}^{S,CL} - b_{2t}^{S+1,CL} \in \{0,1\}$ holds in general. Obviously, this implies $b_{2t}^{S+1,CL} \leq b_{2t}^{S,CL}$ for all $t \geq 0$. Since $b_{2t}^{S+1,CL} \leq b_{2t}^{S,CL}$ implies $B_{2t}^{S+1,CL} \leq_{st} B_{2t}^{S,CL}$, $B_{2t}^{S,CL}$ is stochastically decreasing in S in any period t (Proposition 10).

By Proposition 11, the $(LT+1)$-dimensional Markov chain is ergodic. Therefore the Markov chain converges (in the strong sense) against the unique limit distribution independent of the initial state (see Definition 2 and Theorem 1, also (Borovkov 2003, p. 103)). By Equation (??) $\Pr(B_{2t}^{S,CL} = b_2)$ is computed as the sum over all potential demands of the last LT periods. As convergence is preserved under addition, we have $\lim_{t\to\infty} \Pr(B_{2t}^{S,CL} = b_2) = \Pr(B_2^{S,CL} = b_2)$ and hence $\lim_{t\to\infty} F_t^{S,CL}(x) = F^{S,CL}(x)$. Thus $F_t^{S+1,CL}(x) \geq F_t^{S,CL}(x), \forall x \geq 0, t \geq 1$ implies $F^{S+1,CL}(x) \geq F^{S,CL}(x), \forall x \geq 0$ (Proposition 9). This completes the proof w.r.t. S. The proof for CL can be derived analogously. □

Proof of Proposition 13.

To prove the statement for $B_1^{S,CL}$ w.r.t. S we will show that $b_{1t}^{S,CL} = [d_{1t} - S + io_t - b_{2t-1}^{S,CL}]^+ \geq [d_{1t} - S - 1 + io_t - b_{2t-1}^{S+1,CL}]^+ = b_{1t}^{S+1,CL}$ for any realizations d_{1t}, io_t and any period t. As in Proposition 12, everything else then follows. In the proof of Proposition 12 we have seen that either $b_{2t}^{S,CL} = b_{2t}^{S+1,CL}$ or $b_{2t}^{S,CL} - b_{2t}^{S+1,CL} = 1$ for all $t \geq 0$. If $b_{2t-1}^{S,CL} = b_{2t-1}^{S+1,CL} + 1$, then $d_{1t} - S + io_t - b_{2t-1}^{S,CL} = d_{1t} - S - 1 + io_t - b_{2t-1}^{S+1,CL}$ and hence $b_{1t}^{S,CL} = [d_{1t} - S + io_t - b_{2t-1}^{S,CL}]^+ = [d_{1t} - S - 1 + io_t - b_{2t-1}^{S+1,CL}]^+ = b_{1t}^{S+1,CL}$. If $b_{2t-1}^{S,CL} = b_{2t-1}^{S+1,CL}$, then $d_{1t} - S + io_t - b_{2t}^{S,CL} > d_{1t} - S - 1 + io_t - b_{2t}^{S+1,CL}$. Hence $b_{1t}^{S,CL} = [d_{1t} - S + io_t - b_{2t-1}^{S,CL}]^+$

$\geq [d_{1t} - S - 1 + io_t - b_{2t-1}^{S+1,CL}]^+ = b_{1t}^{S+1,CL}$ for all $t \geq 0$. Therefore, the claim holds for changes in S.
Concerning changes in CL the proof is easier: By Proposition 12, $B_2^{S,CL} \leq_{st} B_2^{S,CL+1}$. Thus $-B_2^{S,CL} \geq_{st} -B_2^{S,CL+1}$ and hence $D_1 - S + IO - B_2^{S,CL} \geq_{st} D_1 - S + IO - B_2^{S,CL+1}$ (Proposition 8). Now the maximum operator is non-decreasing. Therefore, also by Proposition 8, stochastic ordering is preserved under its application. □

Proof of Proposition 14.

By Equations (8.4) and (8.3), the on-hand inventory at the end of a period t for arbitrary demand realizations d_t and io_t is given by

$$ih_t^{S,CL} = S - io_t - d_t + b_{1t}^{S,CL} + b_{2t}^{S,CL}$$

Increasing S to $S+1$, we have $ih_t^{S,CL} = S - io_t - d_t + b_{1t}^{S,CL} + b_{2t}^{S,CL} \leq S + 1 - io_t - d_t + b_{1t}^{S+1,CL} + b_{2t}^{S+1,CL} = ih_t^{S+1,CL}$, because $b_{1t}^{S,CL} + b_{2t}^{S,CL} - b_{1t}^{S+1,CL} - b_{2t}^{S+1,CL} \leq 1$. The latter can be seen by extending the proof of Proposition 12 accordingly.

The proof concerning changes in CL uses the following Lemma:

Lemma 1 *Increasing CL by 1, the decrease in class 1 backorders is smaller than the increase in class 2 backorders, i.e.,* $B_1^{S,CL} - B_1^{S,CL+1} \leq_{st} B_2^{S,CL+1} - B_2^{S,CL}$.

We then have $IH^{S,CL} = S - IO - D + B_1^{S,CL} + B_2^{S,CL} \leq_{st} S - IO - D + B_1^{S,CL+1} + B_2^{S,CL+1} = IH^{S,CL+1}$. □

Proof of Lemma 1.

$B_1^{S,CL} - B_1^{S,CL+1}$ and $B_2^{S,CL+1} - B_2^{S,CL}$ are r.v.s. Therefore we may argue as in the proof of Proposition 12 to show that $B_1^{S,CL} - B_1^{S,CL+1} \leq_{st} B_2^{S,CL+1} - B_2^{S,CL}$. As before, the behavior of the expectations then follows (Proposition 7).

Base case: We start in period $t = 1$. Demands in previous periods are zero. Obviously, $b_{20}^{S,CL+1} = b_{20}^{S,CL} = 0$. Under those conditions Equation (8.5) can be written as

$$b_{11}^{S,CL} = [d_{11} - S]^+ \tag{8.9}$$

Thus $b_{11}^{S,CL} - b_{11}^{S,CL+1} = 0$. For class 2 backorders, either $b_{21}^{S,CL+1} - b_{21}^{S,CL} = 0$ or $b_{21}^{S,CL+1} - b_{21}^{S,CL} = 1$ (cf. proof of Proposition 12 and Equation (8.6)- class 2 backorders react to increases in CL in the same way as to decreases in S). Therefore $b_{11}^{S,CL} - b_{11}^{S,CL+1} \leq b_{21}^{S,CL+1} - b_{21}^{S,CL}$ holds in general.

Induction hypothesis: Assume that in period $t-1$ we have $b_{1t-1}^{S,CL} - b_{1t-1}^{S,CL+1} \leq b_{2t-1}^{S,CL+1} - b_{2t-1}^{S,CL}$.

Induction step: To prove that $b_{1t}^{S,CL} - b_{1t}^{S,CL+1} \leq b_{2t}^{S,CL+1} - b_{2t}^{S,CL}$, we analyze Equation (8.5) for arbitrary demand realizations d_{1t} and io_t, i.e.,

$$b_{1t}^{S,CL} = [d_{1t} - S + io_t - b_{2t-1}^{S,CL}]^+, \tag{8.10}$$

and Equation (8.8). We look at the same three cases as in the proof of Proposition 12.

Case 1: $b_{2t}^{S,CL}$ and $b_{2t}^{S,CL+1}$ are computed by part (A) of Equation (8.8). So, $b_{2t}^{S,CL+1} - b_{2t}^{S,CL} = [d_{1t} + d_{2t} - S + io_t + CL + 1]^+ - [d_{1t} + d_{2t} - S + io_t + CL]^+$. Thus either $b_{2t}^{S,CL+1} = b_{2t}^{S,CL} = 0$ or $b_{2t}^{S,CL+1} - b_{2t}^{S,CL} = 1$. The condition of part (A) of Equation (8.8) implies that $d_{1t} - S + io_t - b_{2t-1}^{S,CL} < -CL$ resp. $d_{1t} - S + io_t - b_{2t-1}^{S,CL+1} < -CL - 1$. Thus $b_{1t}^{S,CL} = b_{1t}^{S,CL+1} = 0$.

Case 2: $b_{2t}^{S,CL}$ is computed by part (A) and $b_{2t}^{S,CL+1}$ is computed by part (B) of Equation (8.8). The condition of part (A) may be re-written as $d_{1t} - S + io_t + CL < b_{2t-1}^{S,CL}$. So, this case only applies if $b_{2t-1}^{S,CL} = b_{2t-1}^{S,CL+1}$ and $d_{1t} - S + io_t + CL = b_{2t-1}^{S,CL} - 1$. Then, $b_{2t}^{S,CL+1} - b_{2t}^{S,CL} = b_{2t-1}^{S,CL} + d_{2t} - [b_{2t-1}^{S,CL} - 1 + d_{2t}]^+$ and $b_{2t}^{S,CL+1} - b_{2t}^{S,CL} = 1$ or $b_{2t}^{S,CL} = b_{2t}^{S,CL+1} = 0$. Now $d_{1t} - S + io_t + CL = b_{2t-1}^{S,CL} - 1$ implies $d_{1t} - S + io_t - b_{2t-1}^{S,CL} = -CL - 1 < 0$ and also $d_{1t} - S + io_t - b_{2t-1}^{S,CL+1} = -CL - 1 < 0$. Hence, by Equation (8.10) $b_{1t}^{S,CL} = b_{1t}^{S,CL+1} = 0$.

Case 3: $b_{2t}^{S,CL}$ and $b_{2t}^{S,CL+1}$ are computed by part (B) of Equation (8.8). In this case $b_{2t}^{S,CL+1} - b_{2t}^{S,CL} = b_{2t-1}^{S,CL+1} - b_{2t-1}^{S,CL}$. If $b_{2t-1}^{S,CL+1} - b_{2t-1}^{S,CL} = 1$, then $b_{1t}^{S,CL} - b_{1t}^{S,CL+1} = [d_{1t} - S + io_t - b_{2t-1}^{S,CL}]^+ - [d_{1t} - S + io_t - b_{2t-1}^{S,CL} - 1]^+$ and $b_{1t}^{S,CL} - b_{1t}^{S,CL+1} = 1$ or $b_{1t}^{S,CL} = b_{1t}^{S,CL+1} = 0$. If $b_{2t-1}^{S,CL+1} = b_{2t-1}^{S,CL}$, then $b_{1t}^{S,CL} - b_{1t}^{S,CL+1} = 0$ by Equation (8.10).

Thus in any period t, we have $b_{1t}^{S,CL} - b_{1t}^{S,CL+1} \leq b_{2t}^{S,CL+1} - b_{2t}^{S,CL}$. □

Proof of Corollary 2.

This is an immediate consequence of Propositions 12 to 14 and Proposition 7. □

Chapter 9

Prioritization by Penalty Costs

We now apply the results of Section 8 to optimize the inventory system if backorders are penalized by costs. Backorder penalty cost of class 1 demand is p_1 and backorder penalty cost of class 2 demand is p_2. Without loss of generality we assume that $p_1 > p_2$. Our performance measure is the expected total cost per period,

$$ETC = h\ EIH + p_1\ EB_1 + p_2\ EB_2. \tag{9.1}$$

The decision variables are the order-up-to level S and the critical level CL.

We will develop an efficient numerical solution algorithm to find the optimal constellation of base stock and critical level (Section 9.1). This solution algorithm will then be applied to a variety of situations to show the advantage of our constant critical level policy compared to traditional inventory policies (Section 9.2). We will also provide a heuristic approach. In Section 9.3, we conclude. The last section of this chapter, Section 9.4, contains all proofs.

K. Möllering, *Inventory Rationing*, Edition KWV,
https://doi.org/10.1007/978-3-658-24255-8_9

9.1 Optimization Approach

We will show that the objective function 9.1 is convex in CL if we choose $S = k+CL$ for a given value of k. We then use this property to derive an efficient solution algorithm. In the algorithm, the objective function value must be computed repetitively. We show how the transition matrix of the underlying Markov chain can be constructed and how the steady state probabilities of the Markov chain can be computed such that the objective function value can be computed efficiently. Finally, we summarize the algorithm.

9.1.1 Convexity of Objective Function

Ideally, we would like to prove joint convexity of the objective function in S and CL or at least convexity of the cost function in S or CL. Unfortunately, Figure 8.1 shows that for small values of S the expected amount of class 1 backorders is **not** convex in S for given CL. In this case, assuming $p_2 = h = 0$ the cost function is also not convex in S for fixed CL. Thus we cannot base our optimization approach on results such as joint convexity in S and CL. However, we can prove the convexity result stated in Proposition 15.

Proposition 15 *Let Z_k^{CL}, $k = 0, 1, \ldots$ denote the expected cost of an inventory system with order-up-to level $S = k + CL$ and critical level CL. Then, for a given value of k, Z_k^{CL} is convex in CL.*

Figure 9.1 illustrates how S depends on CL for a given value of k. Since Z_k^{CL} is convex in CL, we can use any standard optimization approach for finding the critical level that minimizes Z_k^{CL} for fixed k. We denote this critical value by CL_k^*. We determine the optimal expected costs and critical levels for $k = 0, 1, ..., S^{NV}$ and choose the solution with the lowest cost as the solution to our optimization problem, i.e.,

$$Z^* = \min_{k=0,1,\ldots,S^{NV}} Z_k^{CL_k^*}.$$

If we choose S^{NV} such that the optimal solution is not excluded from the search, Z^* is the optimal solution. Proposition 16 states how S^{NV} can be chosen to ensure that the optimal solution is not excluded.

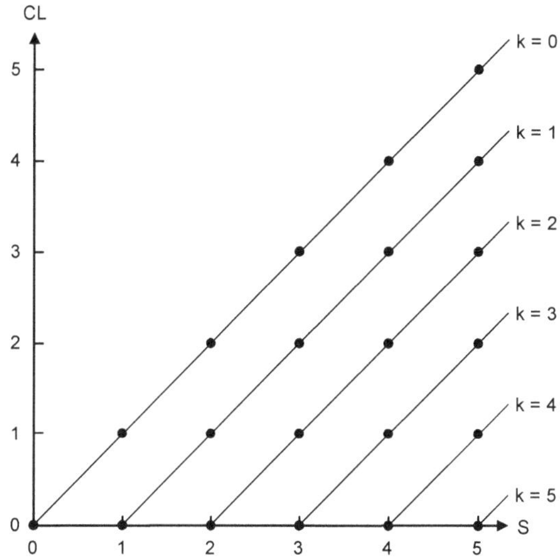

Figure 9.1: Concept of diagonals

Proposition 16 *Let* $S^{NV} = F^{-1}_{D^{LT+1}}\left(\frac{p_1}{p_1+h}\right)$, *where* $F^{-1}_{D^{LT+1}}(\cdot)$ *denotes the inverse of the c.d.f. of the demand over* $LT+1$ *periods. Then, the optimal solution is either* $(S^{NV}, 0)$ *or* $(k + CL, CL)$ *with* $k < S^{NV}$.

The upper limit on k used in Proposition 16, i.e., S^{NV}, is the solution to the standard multi-period newsvendor problem with backorder penalty cost p_1 and inventory holding cost h (see Section 3.3.2). The basic idea behind the computation of S^{NV} is to increase class 2 penalty cost from p_2 to p_1. Then, a critical level of zero is optimal because both customer classes are of equal priority and the resulting inventory system differs from the standard multi-period newsvendor system only in the sequence in which orders are filled. Since the sequence in which we fill orders does not affect costs if $p_2 = p_1$, the optimal order-up-to level is the same as the optimal solution to the multi-period newsvendor problem. This solution can be easily computed and serves as an upper bound on k.

9.1.2 Transition Matrix

In Section 8.3, we have shown how the inventory system can be modeled using a Markov chain with an infinite state space and how the optimal solution can be computed theoretically. What remains to be shown is how the actual computations can be performed. Our approach is to first compute the steady state probabilities of the Markov chain. Based on this distribution, we compute the distribution of class 2 and then of class 1 backorders. Then, we compute expected class 1 and class 2 backorder levels, expected on-hand inventory level, and finally expected cost.

As discussed in Section 5.1.1, directly computing the steady state probabilities from transition matrices with an infinite state space either analytically or numerically requires the presence of some special properties. These special properties are not present in our transition matrix. Therefore, we have to truncate and augment the matrix and compute the steady state probabilities of the truncated matrix (see Section 5.2).

We denote the truncation values for each element of the state space by $b_{2t-1}^{\max}$, $d_{t-1}^{\max}$, ..., $d_{t-LT}^{\max}$. We rely on Equation (8.6) to compute the transition probabilities $p_{x_t,x_{t+1}} = \Pr(X_{t+1} = x_{t+1} = (b_{2t}, d_t, d_{t-1}, \ldots, d_{t-LT+1}) \mid X_t = x_t = (b_{2t-1}, d_{t-1}, d_{t-2}, \ldots, d_{t-LT}))$. Algorithm 2 shows how the transition matrix is computed.

Algorithm 2 The transition matrix is computed as follows:

Initialize $P = 0$

For $b_{2t-1} = 0$ to $b_{2t-1}^{\max}$

For $d_{t-1} = 0$ to $d_{t-1}^{\max}$

...

For $d_{t-LT} = 0$ to $d_{t-LT}^{\max}$

For $d_{1t} = 0$ to $d_t^{\max}$

For $d_{2t} = 0$ to $d_t^{\max} - d_{1t}$

Compute b_{2t} by Equation (8.6)

$p_{(b_{2t-1},d_{t-1},d_{t-2},\ldots,d_{t-LT}),(b_{2t},d_{1t}+d_{2t},d_{t-1},\ldots,d_{t-LT+1})}$

$$+ = f_1(d_{1t})f_2(d_{2t})$$

Return P

Choosing a reasonable value for the truncation limits is important. Small truncation values can result in inaccurate results. Large truncations values can result in long runtimes. We chose the truncation limit for the demand such that the probability mass of all demands that are not considered in the truncated matrix is less than ϵ, i.e., such that $\sum_{d>N} f(d) < \epsilon$, where $f(d)$ denotes the p.d.f. of the demand in a period. For the truncation of class 2 backorders, we used the same N value as for the demand. In our numerical experiments, we used $\epsilon = 10^{-10}$. We apply last column augmentation.

9.1.3 Cost Function

We can use the augmented transition matrix to solve the equation system $\pi P = \pi$ to obtain the steady state probabilities. An efficient and exact algorithm for aperiodic Markov chains like ours is the partitioning algorithm of Sheskin (see Section 5.3). This algorithm repeatedly partitions the transition matrix creating a sequence of smaller transition matrices. The components of the steady state probabilities are then computed starting from the smallest transition matrix.

Once we have computed the steady state probabilities of the Markov chain, it is straightforward to compute the distribution of class 2 backorders by

$$\Pr(B_2 = b_2) = \sum_{d_{t-1}=0}^{N} \cdots \sum_{d_{t-LT}=0}^{N} \Pr(X = x = (b_2, d_{t-1}, ..., d_{t-LT})), \quad (9.2)$$

and hence the expectation of class 2 backorders by

$$EB_2 = \sum_{b_2=0}^{N} b_2 \Pr(B_2 = b_2) \quad (9.3)$$

The long-term expectation of backorders of class 1 is calculated by

$$EB_1 = \sum_{b_2=0}^{N} \sum_{d_{t-1}=0}^{N} \cdots \sum_{d_{t-LT}=0}^{N} (E(B_1|X = x = (b_2, d_{t-1}, ..., d_{t-LT})) \Pr(X = x = (b_2, d_{t-1}, ..., d_{t-LT}))) \quad (9.4)$$

with

$$E(B_1|X = x = (b_2, d_{t-1}, ..., d_{t-LT})) = \sum_{d_1=S-\sum_{i=1}^{LT} d_{t-i}+b_2}^{\infty} (d_1 - S + \sum_{i=1}^{LT} d_{t-i} - b_2) \Pr(D_1 = d_1) \quad (9.5)$$

9.1.4 Numerical Optimization Algorithm

We compute the optimal solution (S^*, CL^*) iteratively based on Proposition 15. Because the cost function Z_k^{CL} is convex in CL we can efficiently search for the cost minimum for all k, $k = 0, 1, \ldots, S^{NV}$. Out of the $S^{NV} + 1$ solutions the solution with the lowest cost is the optimal solution to our optimization problem. Algorithm 3 shows how we compute the optimal solution.

Algorithm 3 The optimization algorithm works as follows:

1. Initialize the algorithm with $k = 0$, $CL_0 = 0$, and $S_0 = 0$. Compute S^{NV}.
2. Calculate $Z_k^{CL_k+1}$.
3. If $Z_k^{CL_k} - Z_k^{CL_k+1} > 0$, set $CL_k = CL_k + 1$ and go to step 2. Else, set $CL_k^* = CL_k$ and $S_k^* = k + CL_k$ and go to step 4.
4. If $k < S^{NV}$, set $k = k + 1$, $S_k = k$ and $CL_k = 0$. Else, let $k^* = \arg\min_{k=0,1,\ldots,S^{NV}} Z_k^{CL_k^*}$, $S^* = k^* + CL_{k^*}^*$, $CL^* = CL_{k^*}^*$ and terminate the algorithm.

Figure 9.2 illustrates the approach for an example with Poisson demands with demand rates $\lambda_1 = 0.75$, $\lambda_2 = 1.25$, lead time $LT = 0$, penalty costs $p_1 = 100$, $p_2 = 10$, and inventory holding cost $h = 1$.

9.2 Numerical Results

We now use our optimization approach for solving a variety of problems. We compare the performance of the critical level policy against the per-

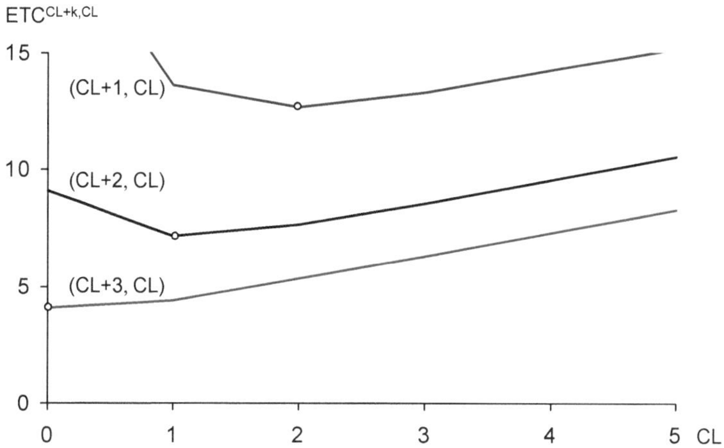

Figure 9.2: Expected total cost per period along different diagonals

formance of two benchmark policies and show that the critical level policy performs significantly better than the benchmark policies. However, computing the optimal parameter values of the critical level policy requires an implementation of our algorithm, which is more complex than computing optimal solutions in traditional inventory systems. Therefore, we develop a simple heuristic that is very easy to implement and show that it performs reasonably well, i.e., better than the benchmark policies, but worse than the optimal policy.

9.2.1 Critical Level Policy versus Benchmark Policies

We compare the critical level policy against two policies without rationing. The first benchmark policy, which we refer to as the *aggregation policy* (AP), treats all demands equally. It uses a common inventory for both demand classes and fills demands and backorders first-come first-serve. This inventory policy is currently in place at the mobile phone company that inspired our research. The average penalty cost under this policy is $\overline{p} = \frac{p_1 ED_1 + p_2 ED_2}{ED_1 + ED_2}$

and the optimal order-up-to level is

$$S^{AP} = F^{-1}_{D^{LT+1}}\left(\frac{\bar{p}}{\bar{p}+h}\right).$$

The second benchmark policy, which we refer to as the *separation policy* (SP), treats both demand classes separately and holds individual inventory for each demand class. This inventory policy is also used by Deshpande et al. (2003) as a benchmark. The optimal order-up-to levels under this policy are

$$S_1^{SP} = F^{-1}_{D_1^{LT+1}}\left(\frac{p_1}{p_1+h}\right) \text{ and } S_2^{SP} = F^{-1}_{D_2^{LT+1}}\left(\frac{p_2}{p_2+h}\right).$$

We denote the sum of the order-up-to levels by $S^{SP} = S_1^{SP} + S_2^{SP}$.

To compare the performances of the policies and to gain insight into the effect of the parameter values on the optimal order-up-to level and optimal critical level, we analyze a variety of parameter value combinations. Without loss of generality, we set $h = 1$. We define a base-case with penalty cost $p_1 = 100$, $p_2 = 10$, Poisson distributed demands with demand rates $\lambda_1 = \lambda_2 = 1.0$, and a lead time of $LT = 1$. Then, we vary each parameter value and analyze the impact of the change on order-up-to levels, critical levels, and cost. The results are shown in Table 9.1.

From Table 9.1 we conclude that the critical level policy significantly outperforms both the aggregation and the separation policy. Between the two benchmark policies, the aggregation policy performs much better than the separation policy, because the aggregation policy can take advantage of risk-pooling while the separation policy cannot. Based on the numerical results, we can also see for which parameter value combinations the performance gap between the critical level policy and the aggregation policy is particularly high: If class 1 penalty cost is high or if class 2 penalty cost is low, the critical level policy performs much better than the aggregation policy.

The numerical results also show that a critical level of $CL = 0$ is optimal in most situations. Only if class 1 penalty cost is very high or class 2 penalty cost is very low, a critical level of greater than zero is optimal. This observation has an important implication, because it motivates the development of a simple heuristic, the combination heuristic, that we present next.

Table 9.1: Critical Level Policy vs. Benchmark Policies - Penalty Cost

	Parameter Values						Critical Level Policy			Aggregation Policy			Separation Policy		
	h	p_1	p_2	λ_1	λ_2	LT	S*	CL*	ETC*	S*	ETC*	% Gap	S*	ETC*	% Gap
BC	1	100	10	1	1	1	8	0	4.651	9	5.687	22.26%	10	7.425	59.63%
Vary h	0.01						12	0	0.085	13	0.096	12.25%	17	0.139	62.65%
	0.1						10	0	0.666	11	0.771	15.82%	14	1.089	63.59%
	1						8	0	4.651	9	5.687	22.26%	10	7.425	59.63%
	10						5	0	23.299	6	32.703	40.36%	6	39.092	67.79%
	100						2	0	61.155	3	108.940	78.14%	2	128.268	109.74%
Vary p_1		10					7	0	3.932	7	3.932	0.00%	8	5.653	43.76%
		100					8	0	4.651	9	5.687	22.26%	10	7.425	59.63%
		1000					9	1	6.028	11	7.654	26.97%	12	9.121	51.31%
		10000					11	1	7.577	13	9.514	25.56%	13	10.391	37.13%
Vary p_2			1				7	1	3.951	9	5.632	42.55%	8	5.681	43.80%
			5				7	0	4.380	9	5.656	29.12%	9	6.906	57.66%
			10				8	0	4.651	9	5.687	22.26%	10	7.425	59.63%
			50				9	0	5.673	9	5.932	4.56%	11	8.745	54.14%
			100				9	0	6.239	9	6.239	0.00%	12	9.197	47.42%
Vary λ_1				0.1			4	0	3.089	5	3.470	12.36%	6	4.749	53.74%
				0.5			6	0	3.783	7	4.705	24.36%	8	6.266	65.62%
				1			8	0	4.651	9	5.687	22.26%	10	7.425	59.63%
				5			19	0	8.864	20	10.013	12.95%	22	12.182	37.43%
Vary λ_2					0.1		6	0	4.569	6	4.731	3.54%	7	5.604	22.65%
					0.5		7	0	4.584	7	5.221	13.90%	8	6.738	47.01%
					1		8	0	4.651	9	5.687	22.26%	10	7.425	59.63%
					5		17	0	6.594	18	8.135	23.36%	20	10.655	61.58%
Vary LT						1	8	0	4.651	9	5.687	22.26%	10	7.425	59.63%
						2	10	0	5.705	12	6.819	19.52%	13	9.015	58.02%
						3	13	0	6.611	14	7.783	17.74%	16	10.171	53.85%
						4	16	0	7.243	17	8.551	18.06%	19	13.799	90.52%

9.2.2 Combination Heuristic

The numerical results not only show that a critical level of zero is often optimal, but also show that the order-up-to levels of the critical level policy and aggregate policy have similar values. In our experiments, the order-up-to levels of the aggregation policy and the critical level policy differ by at most two units. In our combination heuristic, we combine the simplicity of the order-up-to level computation of the aggregation policy with the sequence of events of the critical level policy. More precisely, we compute the order-up-to level with the aggregation policy and use this order-up-to level to execute a critical level policy with critical level $CL = 0$.

Table 9.2 compares the performance of the combination heuristic with the performance of the critical level policy and the aggregation policy. It shows that the performance of the combination heuristic is higher than the performance of the aggregation policy, but that it is still significantly below the performance of the critical level policy. The heuristic performs reasonably well in most cases, often decreasing the gap between the critical level policy and the aggregation policy by more than 50 %. If class 1 and class 2 penalty cost are similar, the heuristic performs quite well. However, it performs poorly if the difference in penalty costs of the two demand classes is high.

We conclude that the combination heuristic achieves a significant performance gain over the aggregate policy while it is almost as simple to implement as the aggregation policy. However, the critical level policy still offers significant performance advantages over the combination heuristic.

9.3 Conclusion

In this chapter, we have analyzed a threshold inventory rationing policy in a periodic review setting with general (constant) lead times, general discrete demand distributions, and optimal backorder clearing. To derive structural properties of the inventory system and to derive an optimal solution algorithm, we modeled the inventory system based on a Markov chain and used a sample path approach for proving several properties of expected backorder levels, inventory level, and cost. We conducted numerical experiments that

Table 9.2: Combination euristic vs. Critical Level Policy an Aggregation Policy - Penalty Cost

	Parameter Values						Critical Level Policy			Combination euristic				Aggregation Policy		
	h	p_1	p_2	λ_1	λ_2	LT	S*	CL*	ETC*	S*	CL*	ETC*	% Gap	S*	ETC*	% Gap
BC	1	100	10	1	1	1	8	0	4.651	9	0	5.221	12.25%	9	5.687	22.26%
Vary h	0.01						12	0	0.085	13	0	0.091	7.20%	13	0.096	12.25%
	0.1						10	0	0.666	11	0	0.719	8.01%	11	0.771	15.82%
	1						8	0	4.651	9	0	5.221	12.25%	9	5.687	22.26%
	10						5	0	23.299	6	0	26.082	11.94%	6	32.703	40.36%
	100						2	0	61.155	3	0	67.249	9.97%	3	108.940	78.14%
Vary p_1		10					7	0	3.932	7	0	3.932	0.00%	7	3.932	0.00%
		100					8	0	4.651	9	0	5.221	12.25%	9	5.687	22.26%
		1000					9	1	6.028	11	0	7.082	17.48%	11	7.654	26.97%
		10000					11	1	7.577	13	0	9.036	19.25%	13	9.514	25.56%
Vary p_2			1				7	1	3.951	9	0	5.120	29.59%	9	5.632	42.55%
			5				7	0	4.380	9	0	5.165	17.91%	9	5.656	29.12%
			10				8	0	4.651	9	0	5.221	12.25%	9	5.687	22.26%
			50				9	0	5.673	9	0	5.673	0.00%	9	5.932	4.56%
			100				9	0	6.239	9	0	6.239	0.00%	9	6.239	0.00%
Vary λ_1				0.1			4	0	3.089	5	0	3.209	3.89%	5	3.470	12.36%
				0.5			6	0	3.783	7	0	4.249	12.32%	7	4.705	24.36%
				1			8	0	4.651	9	0	5.221	12.25%	9	5.687	22.26%
				5			19	0	8.864	20	0	8.960	1.07%	20	10.013	12.95%
Vary λ_2					0.1		6	0	4.569	6	0	4.569	0.00%	6	4.731	3.54%
					0.5		7	0	4.584	7	0	4.584	0.00%	7	5.221	13.90%
					1		8	0	4.651	9	0	5.221	12.25%	9	5.687	22.26%
					5		17	0	6.594	18	0	6.899	4.62%	18	8.135	23.36%
Vary LT						1	8	0	4.651	9	0	5.221	12.25%	9	5.687	22.26%
						2	10	0	5.705	12	0	6.297	10.39%	12	6.819	19.52%
						3	13	0	6.611	14	0	6.700	1.35%	14	7.783	17.74%
						4	16	0	7.243	17	0	7.620	5.21%	17	8.551	18.06%

showed that the critical level policy performs significantly better than traditional inventory policies, in particular, if the difference between the penalty costs of the two demand classes is high. The numerical experiments indicated that a critical level of zero is often optimal. They also indicated that the optimal order-up-to level of the critical level policy can be roughly approximated by the optimal order-up-to level of the aggregation policy, which motivated the development of our combination heuristic that is very easy to implement and yields reasonable results.

The inventory policy we analyzed in this chapter is optimal for inventory systems with a constant critical level. Most likely, an inventory system with a critical level that depends on the entire state of the system will perform better than a constant critical level policy. Finding an optimal policy might be analytically intractable, but finding a policy that contains some elements that are likely to be present in an optimal policy might not. For instance, it is reasonable to assume that the optimal policy will use a higher critical level if only a few replenishments will arrive in the near future than if many will arrive, given the total number of outstanding orders is the same in both cases.

9.4 Proofs

Proof of Proposition 15.

Convexity in CL along diagonal k holds if

$$ETC^{k+CL,CL} - ETC^{k+CL+1,CL+1} \geq ETC^{k+CL+1,CL+1} - ETC^{k+CL+2,CL+2}.$$

By Equation (9.1) the expected cost $ETC^{\,k+CL,CL}$ is

$$ETC^{\,k+CL,CL} = h\ EIH^{\,k+CL,CL} + p_1\ EB_1^{\,k+CL,CL} + p_2\ EB_2^{\,k+CL,CL}.$$

From Equation (8.4) we know that

$$EIH^{\,k+CL,CL} = k + CL - (LT+1)\ ED + EB_1^{\,k+CL,CL} + EB_2^{\,k+CL,CL}.$$

Since sums preserve convexity, it suffices to prove convexity of $EB_1^{\,k+CL,CL}$ and $EB_2^{\,k+CL,CL}$ in CL to prove convexity of $ETC^{\,k+CL,CL}$ in CL. From

Equation (8.6) we can see that ${EB_2}^{k+CL,CL}$ does not depend on CL and therefore is (trivially) convex in CL. Moreover, $-{EB_2}^{k+CL,CL}$ is also convex in CL. Since the maximum operator preserves convexity (Proposition 8), we can see from Equation (8.5) that ${EB_1}^{k+CL,CL}$ is convex in CL. □

Proof of Proposition 16.

For notational convenience, we define the total expected cost with order-up-to level $S = k + CL$ and critical level CL as

$$\begin{aligned} Z_k(CL) &= ETC^{k+CL,CL} \\ &= h\ EIH^{k+CL,CL} + p_1\ EB_1^{k+CL,CL} + p_2\ EB_2^{k+CL,CL}. \end{aligned}$$

As before, we refer to the corresponding diagonal as diagonal k (cf. Figure 9.1) and to the smallest optimal critical level on that diagonal as CL_k^*. Let

$$Z_k^* = Z(CL_k^*) = \min_{CL_k} Z_k(CL_k).$$

We first consider an inventory system where both, class 1 and class 2 customers, have penalty cost p_1, i.e., $p_2 = p_1$. We refer to this model as the newsvendor model. If $p_2 = p_1$ then the cost difference $ETC^{S,CL+1} - ETC^{S,CL}$ is given by

$$\begin{aligned} & ETC^{S,CL+1} - ETC^{S,CL} \\ = \ & h\ EIH^{S,CL+1} + p_1\ EB_1^{S,CL+1} + p_1\ EB_2^{S,CL+1} \\ & -h\ EIH^{S,CL} - p_1\ EB_1^{S,CL} - p_1\ EB_2^{S,CL} \\ = \ & (h + p_1)\left[EB_1^{S,CL+1} - EB_1^{S,CL} + EB_2^{S,CL+1} - EB_2^{S,CL}\right] \end{aligned}$$

By Lemma 1, $EB_1^{S,CL+1} - EB_1^{S,CL} + EB_2^{S,CL+1} - EB_2^{S,CL} \geq 0$. Thus a critical level of $CL = 0$ is optimal. Since the sequence in which demands and backorders are filled does not affect the cost in this model, the optimal order-up-to level S is the optimal solution of the multi-period newsvendor model,

$$S^{NV} = F_{DLT+1}^{-1}\left(\frac{p_1}{p_1 + h}\right).$$

We denote the cost of this solution as $\tilde{Z}_{S^{NV}}^*$. Because $\tilde{Z}_{S^{NV}}^*$ is the optimal solution, $\tilde{Z}_{S^{NV}}^* \leq \tilde{Z}_k^*$ for $k > S^{NV}$.

Next, we show that an inventory system with the same class 1 penalty cost as above but with lower class 2 penalty cost, i.e., with $p_2 < p_1$, cannot have an optimal solution on diagonals $k > S^{NV}$.

From Equation (8.6) it can be seen that class 2 backorder quantities are the same for all parameter constellations $(k + CL, CL)$ on a diagonal k. Therefore, reductions in p_2 reduce the cost of all parameter constellations $(k + CL, CL)$ on diagonal k by the same amount. This implies that the optimal critical level on a diagonal k is not affected by the value of p_2.

If we reduce class 2 penalty cost from p_1 to p_2, the value of the optimal solution on diagonal $k = S^{NV}$ decreases by $(p_1 - p_2)EB_2^{S^{NV},0}$. The value of the optimal solution on diagonal $k > S^{NV}$ decreases by $(p_1 - p_2)EB_2^{k,CL_k^*} = (p_1 - p_2)EB_2^{k,0}$. Note that $EB_2^{k,CL_k^*} = EB_2^{k,0}$, because the class 2 backorder level is the same for all parameter constellations $(k + CL, CL)$ on diagonal k.

From Corollary 2, we can conclude that $EB_2^{S^{NV},0} \geq EB_2^{k,0}$ for $k > S^{NV}$. So, if we decrease the penalty cost of class 2 from p_1 to p_2, the cost of the optimal solution on diagonal $k = S^{NV}$ decreases by at least the same amount as the cost of the optimal solution on diagonal $k > S^{NV}$, i.e., $(p_1 - p_2)EB_2^{S^{NV},0} \geq (p_1 - p_2)EB_2^{k,0}$. Therefore, $k = S^{NV}$ is an upper bound on the diagonal on which the optimal solution can be located for any $p_2 \leq p_1$.

In particular, we showed that on the diagonal S^{NV} itself, $CL_{S^{NV}}^* = 0$ remains optimal. □

Chapter 10

Prioritization by Service Levels

In contrast to the setting of the previous chapter, the two demand classes are now prioritized based on service requirements. We will start with α-service levels, α_1 and α_2. Without loss of generality, we assume that $\alpha_1 \geq \alpha_2$. Later, we will also study β-service requirements.

Our objective is to analyze the behavior of the policy and optimize the expected total cost per period ETC. Thus we are interested in solving the following minimization problem:

$$\begin{aligned} \min_{S,CL} ETC^{S,CL} &= h\, EIH^{S,CL} \\ s.th.\ \Pr(B_1^{S,CL} = 0) &\geq \alpha_1 \\ \Pr(B_2^{S,CL} = 0) &\geq \alpha_2 \\ S, CL \in \mathbb{N}, S &> CL \end{aligned} \tag{10.1}$$

Again, the decision variables are the order-up-to level S and the critical level CL.

In Section 10.1, we will characterize potentially optimal parameter constellations and derive some structural results concerning the optimal solution and the cost function. A numerical optimization algorithm as well as numerical

K. Möllering, *Inventory Rationing*, Edition KWV,
https://doi.org/10.1007/978-3-658-24255-8_10

results are presented in Section 10.2. In Section 10.3, we conclude. Again, all proofs may be found at the end of this chapter, in Section 10.4.

10.1 Analytical Insights

In this section, we will gain structural insights into the service constraint periodic rationing problem which will form the foundation for the numerical optimization in Section 5. We will derive some structural properties of the service level requirements and the objective function. Based on those properties, we will classify the optimal solutions and characterize the behavior of the optimal cost.

10.1.1 Service Level Constraints

By Equation (8.6), the probability of no stock-outs for class 2 customers in period t is given by

$$\begin{aligned} \Pr(B_{2t}^{S,CL} = 0) &= \Pr(S - IO_t - D_{1t} - D_{2t} \geq CL) \\ &\quad + \Pr(S - IO_t - D_{1t} < CL, B_{2t-1}^{S,CL} = D_{2t} = 0) \end{aligned} \tag{10.2}$$

Proposition 17 states how the the order-up-to level S and the critical level CL affect the class 2 service level in steady state. These results are intuitive, because the more units there are, i.e., the higher S, the less likely a shortage. On the other hand, if less inventory is accessible for class 2 customers, i.e., if CL is increased, then shortage for class 2 customers will become more likely.

Proposition 17 *The α-service level for class 2 customers,* $\Pr(B_2^{S,CL} = 0)$, *is increasing in S and decreasing in CL.*

Proposition 18 states that $\Pr(B_2^{S,CL} = 0)$ does not depend on the individual values of S and CL but only on their difference, $S - CL$.

Proposition 18 $\Pr(B_2^{S,CL} = 0)$ *only depends on the difference $S - CL$, not on the individual values of S and CL, i.e.,* $\Pr(B_2^{S,CL} = 0) = \Pr(B_2^{S+k,CL+k} = 0)$ *for any $k \geq 0$.*

As an immediate consequence of Proposition 18, we conclude that the α-service level constraint $\Pr(B_2^{S,CL} = 0) \geq \alpha_2$ is always fulfilled if the difference between S and CL exceeds a certain value. For notational convenience, given S we define CL_2^S as the minimum critical level that guarantees a service level of α_2, i.e.,

$$CL_2^S = \arg\min_{CL}\{\Pr(B_2^{S,CL} = 0) \geq \alpha_2\}.$$

From Equation (8.5), the class 1 α-service level in period t can be computed as

$$\Pr(B_{1t}^{S,CL} = 0) = \Pr(S - IO_t + B_{2t-1}^{S,CL} - D_{1t} \geq 0). \qquad (10.3)$$

The effect of S and CL on the class 1 service level is summarized Proposition 19.

Proposition 19 *The α-service level for class 1 customers, $\Pr(B_1^{S,CL} = 0)$, is increasing in both, S and CL.*

Proposition 19 states what we would expect: Increases of S or CL increase the availability of inventory for class 1 customers - either for exclusive usage or more stock in general - which reduces the likelihood of a backorder and thus increases the class 1 service level. For notational convenience, given S we define CL_1^S as the minimum critical level that guarantees a service level of α_1, i.e.,

$$CL_1^S = \arg\min_{CL}\{\Pr(B_1^{S,CL} = 0) \geq \alpha_1\}.$$

By Proposition 19, CL_1^S is non-increasing in S as long as defined. However, the set might be empty if (S, S) does not fulfill the service level requirement.

The next proposition characterizes the parameter constellations satisfying the α-service level constraint for class 1 customers.

Proposition 20 *If (S, CL) satisfies the α-service level constraint $\Pr(B_1^{S,CL} = 0) \geq \alpha_1$, so do all parameter constellations (S', CL') with $S' \geq S$ and $CL' \geq CL$. Furthermore, if (S, CL) satisfies the constraint and $(S-1, CL)$ does not, the α-service level constraint may however be satisfied for $(S-1, CL+k), k \geq 1$.*

Obviously, decreasing S by 1 reduces the probability of zero backorders of class 1 customers. However, increasing CL might equal out this decrease. In contrast to the case of class 2 customers, we cannot be more precise about the feasible parameter constellations concerning the required α-service level for class 1 customers. For example, CL_1^S as a function of S might be neither convex nor concave.

We refer to the minimal order-up-to level S satisfying the class 1 or class 2 service level constraint given a zero critical level, i.e., given $CL = 0$, by S_1^0 and S_2^0, respectively. Figure 10.1 shows how the minimum critical levels required by the service level constraints depend on the order-up-to level S for an example with Poisson distributed demands with parameters $\lambda_1 = \lambda_2 = 1.5$, lead time $LT = 2$ and required α-service levels of $\alpha_1 \geq 99\%$ and $\alpha_2 \geq 45\%$. The feasible region is the intersection of the areas above CL_1^S and below CL_2^S. Of course, as we have not made any restrictions on

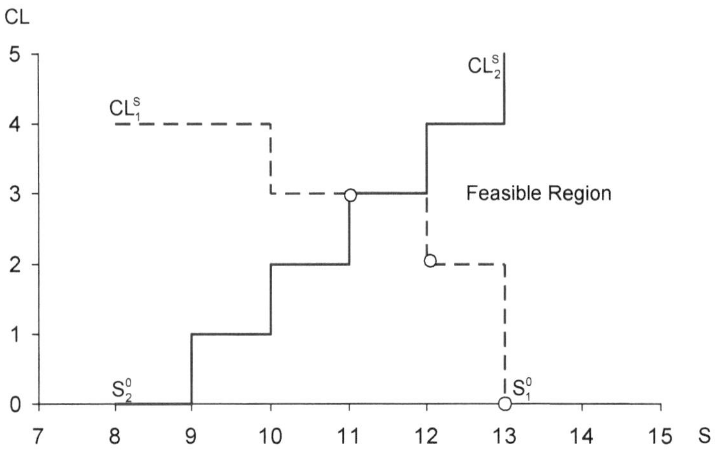

Figure 10.1: Feasible and potentially optimal (S, CL)-pairs

the values of the required α-service levels α_1 and α_2, it might happen that $S_2^0 > S_1^0$.

10.1.2 Potentially Optimal Parameter Constellations

Our objective is to minimize the expected total cost per period. Recall from Section 8.2, that we charge inventory holding cost against the inventory at the end of a period and that the ending inventory of period t is

$$IH_t = I_{t+1} - D_{t-LT}. \tag{10.4}$$

The inventory on hand at the end of a period also equals the inventory at the beginning of the period without the new demands of both classes for the period but including the amount of new backorders of both classes in this period. Applying Equation (8.3), these considerations lead to

$$\begin{aligned} EIH^{S,CL} &= E(S - IO - D_1 - D_2 + B_1^{S,CL} + B_2^{S,CL}) \\ &= S - (LT+1)\left[ED_1 + ED_2\right] + EB_1^{S,CL} + EB_2^{S,CL} \end{aligned} \tag{10.5}$$

From Part 3 of Corollary 2, we know that the inventory on hand at the end of period increases if the order-up-to level S or the rationing level CL increases.

If the two constraints do not meet or meet in one point, then it is an immediate consequence of Corollary 2 that the smallest feasible S is optimal. This is stated in Proposition 21.

Proposition 21 *If $S_2^0 \geq S_1^0$, then the optimal parameter constellation is $(S_2^0, 0)$.*

Note that this case does not mean that the required α-service level for class 1 customers is lower than the one for class 2 customers. The model is constructed in such a way, that for a given parameter constellation the α-service level for class 1 customers is always higher than the α-service level for class 2 customers. If we required the same α-service level for both classes, this would therefore lead to such a situation.

Part 3 of Corollary 2 also allows us to minimize the amount of potentially optimal parameter constellations if the graphs of the functions CL_1^S and CL_2^S intersect. We note that it is possible that $CL_1^S = CL_1^{S'} = k$. In this case, we refer to the smallest order-up-to level S with $CL_1^S = k$ as *likely*.

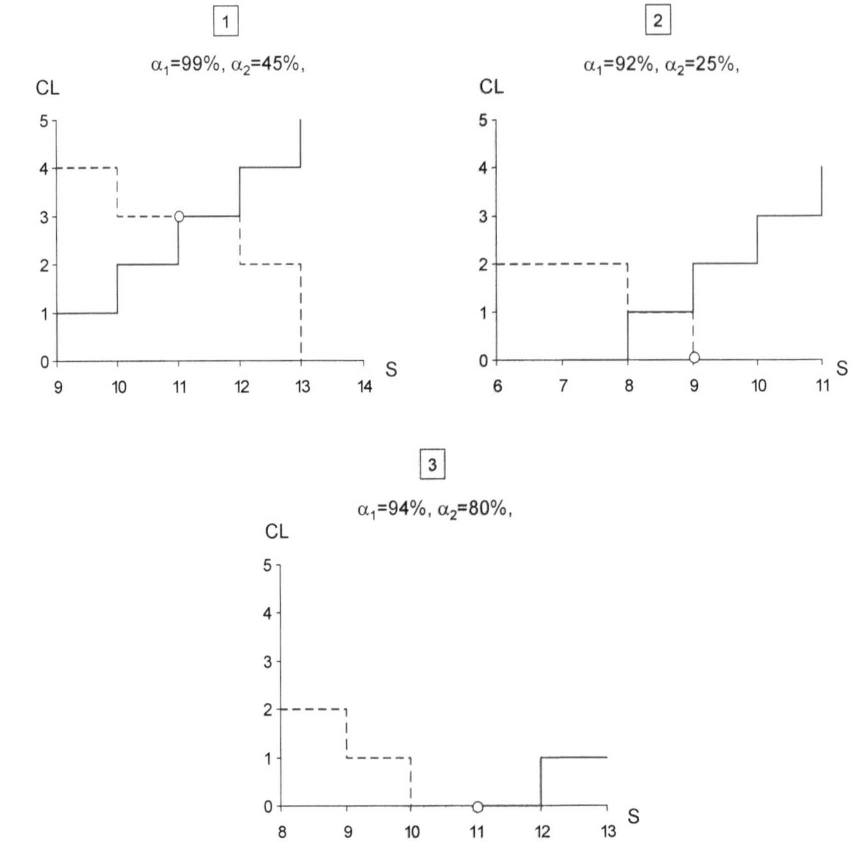

Figure 10.2: Optimal solutions

Proposition 22 *Let* $\Omega = (\max\{S_1^0, S_2^0\}, 0) \cup \{(S, CL_1^S) | CL_2^S \geq CL_1^S \geq 0$ *and* S *likely*$\}$. *Then, the optimal solution is in the set* Ω.

The set Ω coincides with the circled parameter constellations in Figure 10.1. Unfortunately, it is not possible to restrict the set of potentially optimal solutions further Ω than proposed by Proposition 22 - at least, we have not been able to do so. Figure 10.2 provides examples that show that optimal solutions can have various properties: 1. $CL_1^S = CL_2^S = CL^* > 0$, 2. $CL_2^S > CL_1^S = CL^*$, 3. $S_1^0 < S_2^0$, thus $CL_2^{S_2^0} = CL^* = 0$.

In all three cases, demands are Poisson distributed with parameters $\lambda_1 = \lambda_2 = 1.5$. The lead time is $LT = 2$. Table 10.1 lists the service level constraints and the elements ω_i of the respective optimality set Ω for all three examples.

Example	α_1	α_2	ω_i	ETC^{ω_i}
1	99%	45%	$(11,3)$	3.56
			$(12,2)$	3.71
			$(13,0)$	4.16
2	92%	25%	$(8,1)$	1.26
			$(9,0)$	1.19
3	94%	80%	$(11,0)$	2.48

Table 10.1: Optimality sets

10.1.3 Structural Results for the Optimal Solution

The examples in Figure 10.2 and Table 10.1 indicate, that if the required α-service levels are high, especially for class 1 customers, it might be better to go for lower values of S putting up with higher values for CL. For Poisson demands with parameters $\lambda_1 = \lambda_2 = 1.5$ and a lead time $LT = 2$, the optimal solutions for various α-service level combinations are clustered as follows: Either $(S_2^0, 0)$ or $(S_1^0, 0)$ is optimal, or the optimal solution applies a critical level of $CL = 1, 2$ or 3. The result is shown in Figure 10.3. The next proposition states that this behavior of ordered increase in CL can be observed in general.

Proposition 23 *For any required class 1 α-service level α_1 there exists a sequence of threshold service levels $100\% \geq st_0(\alpha_1) \geq st_1(\alpha_1) \geq ... \geq 0\%$ such that for all required class 2 α-service levels α_2 with $st_i(\alpha_1) \geq \alpha_2 > st_{i+1}(\alpha_1)$, the optimal parameter constellation has a critical level of $CL = i$. If $\alpha_2 > st_0(\alpha_1)$, then $(S_2^0, 0)$ is optimal.*

Obviously, the threshold service level $st_0(\alpha_1)$ corresponds to the lowest service level requirement for class 2 customers that leads to $S_2^0 = S_1^0$. Similarly, we may interpret the threshold service level $st_1(\alpha_1)$ as the minimum service

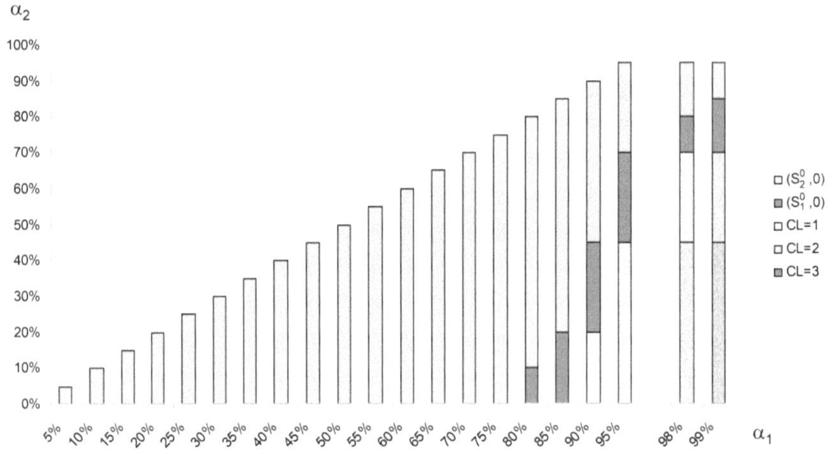

Figure 10.3: Clustered optimal solutions depending on service level requirements

level requirement for class 2 customers leading to an optimal parameter constellation $(S_1^0, 0)$: For a given α-service level α_1 for class 1 customer, this proposition implies that if the required α-service level α_2 is below the threshold service level $st_1(\alpha_1)$, additional cost advantages can only be realized by decreasing S further on the expense of an increased critical level, otherwise the α-service level α_1 is no longer met.

It seems, that the same holds if we fix the required α-service level for class 2 customers instead of that for class 1 customers. However, this is not true. For instance, assuming Poisson demands with $\lambda_1 = 5$ and $\lambda_2 = 1.5$ and a lead time of $LT = 2$, the optimal critical level given α-service requirements of $\alpha_1 = 96\%$ and $\alpha_2 = 80\%$ is 1. If we require $\alpha_1 = 97\%$, the optimal critical level drops to 0. Nonetheless, Proposition 24 states that the threshold service level $st_0(\alpha_1)$ as constructed in the proof of Proposition 23 is non-decreasing in α_1.

Proposition 24 *The threshold service level* $st_0(\alpha_1) := \Pr(B_2^{S_1^0,0} = 0)$ *is non-decreasing in the required* α*-service level* α_1 *for class 1 customers.*

As an immediate consequence of Propositions 23 and 24, a non-zero critical level can only be optimal if the two α-service level constraints are not too close together. This is stated in Corollary 3.

Corollary 3 *If the required α-service level α_1 is not much larger than the required α-service level for class 2 customers, α_2, then a rationing level $CL = 0$ is optimal.*

Ideally, we would be able to calculate all the threshold service level analytically. However, as the backorders levels and α-service levels can only be calculated numerically, this is not possible.

10.1.4 Cost Function

Proposition 23 already indicated that for fixed required α-service level α_1 for class 1 customers there is a threshold service level $st_1(\alpha_1)$ such that for $\alpha_2 < st_1(\alpha_1)$ it is better to gradually increase the critical level CL. We can show the analogous behavior for the order-up-to level S.

Proposition 25 *For any required class 1 α-service level α_1 there exists a sequence of threshold service levels $100\% \geq st'_0(\alpha_1) \geq st'_1(\alpha_1) \geq ... \geq 0\%$ such that for all required class 2 α-service levels α_2 with $st'_i(\alpha_1) \geq \alpha_2 > st'_{i+1}(\alpha_1)$, the optimal parameter constellation has a order-up-to level of $S = S_1^0 - i$. If $\alpha_2 > st'_0(\alpha_1)$, then $(S_2^0, 0)$ is optimal.*

Based on those two results, we may prove analytically that for a fixed required α-service level α_1 for class 1 customers, the optimal expected costs per period ETC^* is increasing in the required α-service level α_2 for class 2 customers.

Proposition 26 *Let the required α-service level α_1 for class 1 customers be fixed. Then the optimal expected total cost per period ETC^* is a step function increasing in the required α-service level for class 2 customers, α_2.*

For Poisson demands with $\lambda_1 = \lambda_2 = 1.5$, a lead time of $LT = 2$ and a required α-service level for class 1 customers of $\alpha_1 = 95\%$, this behavior is shown in Figure 10.4 assuming a holding cost rate $h = 1$.

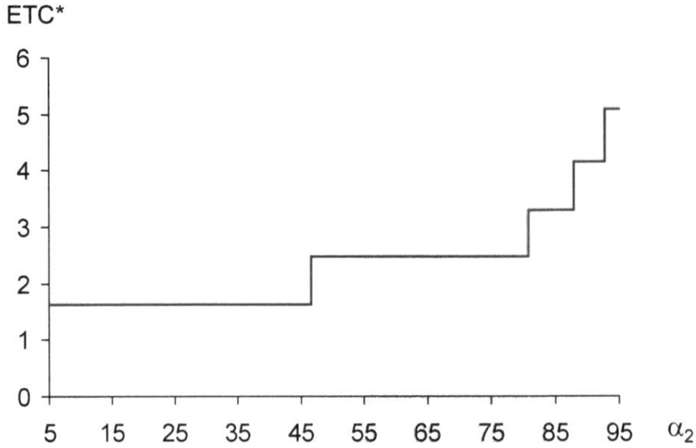

Figure 10.4: Expected optimal costs per period depending on α_2 for fixed α_1

10.1.5 Model Alteration: β-Service Levels

Often, companies are not so much interested in α-service levels but rather require certain fill rates. We will now show that the structural results we gained so far carry over to this case.

In periodic settings, exact loss rates are not easy to calculate and commonly approximated by $\frac{EB}{ED}$ (Thonemann 2005, p.240). The problem we are interested in right now can then be formulated as

$$\begin{aligned} \min_{S,CL} ETC^{S,CL} &= h\ EIH^{S,CL} \\ s.th.\ 1 - \frac{EB_1^{S,CL}}{ED_1} &\geq \beta_1 \\ 1 - \frac{EB_2^{S,CL}}{ED_2} &\geq \beta_2 \\ S, CL &\in \mathbb{N}, S > CL \end{aligned} \tag{10.6}$$

Without loss of generality, we assume that $\beta_1 \geq \beta_2$.

All the structural results concerning the set of potentially optimal parameter constellations, the optimal solution and the cost function are based on the set of feasible parameter constellations as described in Section 4.1. Thus they will also hold for Problem 10.6 if we can show that the overall structure of the set of feasible parameter constellations is analogous to the situation displayed in Figure 10.1.

Proposition 27 states that the fill rates $1 - \frac{EB_1^{S,CL}}{ED_1}$ and $1 - \frac{EB_2^{S,CL}}{ED_2}$ react to changes in S and CL in the same way as the α-service levels (Propositions 17 and 19).

Proposition 27 *For the fill rates the following properties hold:*

1. *The fill rate for class 2 customers,* $1 - \frac{EB_2^{S,CL}}{ED_2}$*, is increasing in* S *and decreasing in* CL*.*
2. *The fill rate for class 1 customers,* $1 - \frac{EB_1^{S,CL}}{ED_1}$*, is increasing in both,* S *and* CL*.*

Equation (8.6) still depends on the difference $S - CL$ only and not on the specific values of the base stock and rationing levels. Consequently, as in the case of α-service levels, the fill rate for class 2 customers depends on this difference only and constraint 2 is linear. Proposition 28 states that the feasible parameter constellations for the class 1 fill rate is limited in the same way as it was given α-service levels.

Proposition 28 *If* (S, CL) *satisfies the fill rate constraint* $1 - \frac{EB_1^{S,CL}}{ED_1} \geq \beta_1$*, so do all parameter constellations* (S', CL') *with* $S' \geq S$ *and* $CL' \geq CL$*. Furthermore, if* (S, CL) *satisfies the fill rate constraint and* $(S-1, CL)$ *does not, the fill rate constraint may however be satisfied for* $(S-1, CL+k), k \geq 1$*.*

Obviously, Part 3 of Corollary 2 also holds for the β-constraint Problem 2 and thus all other structural results follow.

10.2 Numerical Results

In this section, we develop a numerical algorithm for finding the optimal parameter constellation. We then use our optimization approach for solving a variety of problems. We compare the performance of the critical level policy against the performance of two benchmark policies and show that the critical level policy performs significantly better than the benchmark policies. However, computing the optimal parameter values of the critical level policy requires an implementation of our algorithm, which is much more complex than computing optimal solutions in traditional inventory systems. Therefore, we develop a heuristic that is very easy to calculate and show that it performs reasonably well, i.e., much better than the benchmark policy, but worse than the optimal policy.

10.2.1 Optimization Algorithm

As presented in Section 8.3, we take into account the dependence between class 2 backorders and the inventory on order using an $LT+1$-dimensional Markov chain to derive the joint distribution of those r.v.s. This Markov chain may be solved numerically in the same way as outlined in Sections 9.1.2 and 9.1.3: First, we truncate each dimension of the state space, i.e., the transition matrix only includes states with demands and backorders that are smaller than a certain value. Next, we generate the transition matrix applying Algorithm 2. In a third step, we augment this generated matrix, i.e., we set the entries in the last column such that the sum of entries in each row equals 1 again. Eventually, we solve the matrix using Sheskin's algorithm (see Section 5.3). From the joint distribution of the inventory on order and the class 2 backorders, we then derive the expectation of class 1 and class 2 backorders applying Equations (9.2) to (9.5). The on-hand inventory at the end of period EIH follows again from Equation (10.5). Additionally, by Equation (10.3) the α-service level for class 1 customers is calculated by

$$\Pr(B_1=0)=\sum_{b_2=0}^{N}\cdots\sum_{d_{t-LT}=0}^{N}\quad(\Pr(B_1=0|X=x=(b_2,d_{t-1},...,d_{t-LT}))$$
$$\Pr\left(X=x=(b_2,d_{t-1},...,d_{t-LT})\right))$$

with

$$\Pr(B_1=0|X=x=(b_2,d_{t-1},...,d_{t-LT}))=\Pr(S-\sum_{i=1}^{LT}d_{t-i}-D_1+b_2\geq 0).$$

Being able to calculate all those measures, we may now derive the optimal parameter constellation numerically. However, an efficient algorithm that makes use of the knowledge obtained so far requires a sophisticated initialization such as $S = S_2^0$, $CL = 0$. Therefore, we first derive an lower limit for S_2^0.

Let $F_{D^k}(\cdot)$ denote the cumulative distribution function (c.d.f.) for the total demand of k periods, and as usual $\overline{F}(\cdot) = 1 - F(\cdot)$.

Proposition 29 *Define* S_2^{Low} *as* $\min_S\{F_{D^{LT+1}}(S) + \overline{F_{D^{LT}} * f_1}(S)\ f_2(0) \geq \alpha_2\}$. *Then* $S_2^{Low} \leq S_2^0$.

We now propose the following algorithm to find the optimizer (S^*, CL^*) for Problem 10.1: In a first step, we have to find S_2^0 starting from the lower limit S_2^{Low}. Then, we search for the members of the set $\{(S_{CL}, CL)\}$ as defined in Proposition 22. We have to calculate the cost associated with each of those parameter constellations and compare them in the end.

Algorithm 4 The optimization algorithm works as follows:

1. Initialize the algorithm with $S_0 = S_2^{Low}, CL_0 = 0$.

2. Find $S_2^0 := \min\{S \geq S_0 |\ \Pr(B_2^{S,0} = 0) \geq \alpha_2\}$. If $\Pr(B_1^{S_2^0,0} = 0) \geq \alpha_1$, set $(S^*, CL^*) = (S_2^0, 0)$ and terminate the algorithm. Else, go to step 3.

3. Reinitialize the system with $S_{-1} = S_2^0$.

4. If $\Pr(B_1^{S_k,k} = 0) < \alpha_1$, set $S_k = S_k + 1$. Else, set $S_k^* = S_k$, calculate $EIH^{S_k^*,k}$ and go to step 5.

5. If $S_{-1} + k + 1 < S_k^*$, set $S_k = S_{-1} + k + 1$. Else, let $k^* = \arg\min_{k=0,1,\ldots} EIH^{S_k^*,k}$, $S^* = S_{k^*}^*$, $CL^* = k^*$ and terminate the algorithm.

10.2.2 Critical Level Policy versus Benchmark Policies

We again compare the critical level policy against the two policies without rationing that we already used as a benchmark in Section 9.2. The *aggregation policy* (AP), treats all demands equally. It uses a common inventory for both demand classes and fills demands and backorders first-come first-serve. Aiming at the higher service level for all demand independent of its origin, we can ensure that both service constraints are met. The optimal order-up-to level is 2.5:

$$S^{AP} = F^{-1}_{D^{LT+1}}(\alpha_1).$$

The *separation policy* (SP) treats both demand classes separately and holds individual inventory for each demand class. The optimal order-up-to levels under this policy are

$$S_1^{SP} = F^{-1}_{D_1^{LT+1}}(\alpha_1) \text{ and } S_2^{SP} = F^{-1}_{D_2^{LT+1}}(\alpha_2).$$

We denote the sum of the order-up-to levels by $S^{SP} = S_1^{SP} + S_2^{SP}$.

To compare the performance of the policies and to gain insight into the effect of the parameter values on the optimal order-up-to level and optimal critical level, we analyze a variety of parameter value combinations. Without loss of generality, we set $h = 1$. We define a base case with required α-service level $\alpha_1 = 99\%$, $\alpha_2 = 90\%$, Poisson distributed demands with demand rates $\lambda_1 = \lambda_2 = 1.5$, and a lead time of $LT = 2$. Then, we vary each parameter value and analyze the impact of the change on order-up-to level, critical level and cost. The results are shown in Table 10.2.

From Table 10.2, we conclude that the critical level policy significantly outperforms both the aggregation and separation policy. Not surprisingly, the advantage increases with increasing difference in the required α-service levels for the two customers classes, i.e., with increasing $\alpha_1 - \alpha_2$. For the same reason, namely its ability to adapt to the differences in service level requirements, the critical level policy is also particularly advantageous if class 2 customer demand is comparatively high and thus more dominating than class 1 customer demand.

Between the two benchmark policies, the aggregation policy in most cases performs much better than the separation policy, because the aggregation policy can take advantage of risk-pooling while the separation policy cannot. Only for very large differences between the two required α-service levels, the separation policy outperforms the aggregation policy. This is due to the fact

Table 10.2: Critical Level Policy vs. Eenchmark Policies - Service Level

	Parameter Values					Critical Level Policy			Aggregation Policy			Separation Policy		
	1	2	λ_1	λ_2	LT	S*	CL*	ETC*	S*	ETC*	%Gap	S*	ETC*	%Gap
BC	99%	90%	1.5	1.5	2	13	0	4.158	17	8.010	92.63%	17	8.164	96.35%
Vary 1	95%					13	0	4.158	14	5.084	22.27%	15	6.222	49.63%
	96%					13	0	4.158	15	6.043	45.33%	16	7.181	72.72%
	97%					13	0	4.158	15	6.043	45.33%	16	7.181	72.72%
	98%					13	0	4.158	16	7.021	68.85%	16	7.181	72.72%
	99%					13	0	4.158	17	8.010	92.63%	17	8.164	96.35%
Vary 2		70%				12	2	3.703	17	8.010	116.30%	15	6.630	**79.06%**
		80%				13	0	4.158	17	8.010	92.63%	16	7.333	**76.37%**
		90%				13	0	4.158	17	8.010	92.63%	17	8.164	96.35%
		95%				14	0	5.084	17	8.010	57.54%	18	9.078	78.55%
Vary λ_1			0.5			9	0	3.161	12	6.015	90.26%	12	6.160	94.85%
			1			11	0	3.662	15	7.508	105.04%	15	7.659	109.19%
			1.5			13	0	4.158	17	8.010	92.63%	17	8.164	96.35%
			5			27	2	7.816	30	10.523	34.62%	32	12.667	62.06%
Vary λ_2				0.5		11	0	5.035	12	6.015	19.46%	13	7.100	41.02%
				1		12	0	4.582	15	7.508	63.84%	15	7.645	66.83%
				1.5		13	0	4.158	17	8.010	92.63%	17	8.164	96.35%
				5		25	0	5.759	30	10.523	82.71%	30	10.723	86.18%
Vary LT					1	9	0	3.161	12	6.015	90.26%	13	7.140	125.86%
					2	13	0	4.158	17	8.010	92.63%	17	8.164	96.35%
					3	17	0	5.145	21	9.012	75.15%	21	9.176	78.34%
					4	21	0	6.129	25	10.013	63.36%	26	11.169	82.23%

that the latter cannot take into account the comparatively low α-service level α_2 required for class 2 customers.

We also retrieve the result of Corollary 3 concerning an optimal critical level of $CL > 0$. Additionally, the numerical results show that this is also the case if demands for class 1 customers clearly dominate.

10.2.3 Heuristic Approach

The numerical results not only show that a critical level of zero is often optimal, but also indicate that the main reason for the outstanding performance of the critical level policy is its ability to mirror both, the different α-service level requirements for the two customer classes and their different demand patterns. This ability is also incorporated in a order-up-to level policy similar to the aggregation policy but aiming at an average service level, therefore referred to as the *averaging policy* (AV). The required α-service level $\overline{\alpha}$ is calculated by $\overline{\alpha} = \frac{\alpha_1 ED_1 + \alpha_2 ED_2}{ED_1 + ED_2}$ and the optimal order-up-to level by

$$S^{AV} = F^{-1}_{D^{LT+1}}(\overline{\alpha}).$$

In our heuristic, we again combine the simplicity of the order-up-to level computation of this averaging policy and the sequence of events of the critical level policy. More precisely, we compute the order-up-to level with the averaging policy and use this order-up-to level to execute a critical level heuristic with critical level $CL = 0$.

Of course, applying this heuristic we cannot guarantee that the original service level requirements are always met. However, the weighted average of the α-service levels applying the sequence of events of the critical level policy is higher than the α-service level achieved with the optimal order-up-to level without rationing. Treating both customer classes as one, backorders are only zero if both customer classes do not incur a stock out. Under the critical level policy we also take into account those events in which only demand of one customer class cannot be met entirely. For example, assuming the setting of our base case except for a required α-service level for class 2 customers of $\alpha_2 = 70\%$, the lowest order-up-to level fulfilling the average required α-service level is $S^{AV} = 12$. Under a non-rationing policy, this leads to an actual average α-service level of $\overline{\alpha} = 87.6\%$. However, under a critical level policy with parameters $S = 12$ and $CL = 0$ we obtain α-service levels of $\alpha_1 = 98.2\%$ and $\alpha_2 = 87.9\%$ resulting in an average α-service level of $\overline{\alpha} = 93\%$.

Table 10.3 compares the performance of the heuristic with the performance of the critical level policy and the aggregation policy. It shows that the heuristic clearly outperforms the aggregation policy, but that in many cases it still cannot reach the performance of the critical level policy. Remarkably, there is only one case, in which the α-service level requirements are not met, namely when the required α-service level for class 2 customers is lowered to $\alpha_2 = 70\%$.

We conclude that at the risk of not exactly meeting the required α-service level especially for class 1 customers, the heuristic achieves a significant performance gain over the aggregation policy while it is almost as simple to implement.

10.3 Conclusion

In this chapter, we analyzed a threshold inventory rationing policy in a periodic review setting with general (constant) lead times, quite general demand distributions, and optimal backorder clearing. To gain structural insights of the inventory system and to derive an optimal solution algorithm, we first characterized the feasible parameter constellations and narrowed down the choice of potentially optimal parameter constellations. We conducted numerical experiments that showed that the critical level policy performs significantly better than traditional inventory policies, in particular, if the difference between the required α-service levels of the two demand classes is high. The numerical experiments indicated that a critical level of zero is often optimal. They also indicated that the optimal order-up-to level of the critical level policy can be roughly approximated by the optimal order-up-to level of the averaging policy, which motivated the development of our heuristic that is very easy to implement and yields reasonable results.

In contrast to service-constraint inventory policies with only one customer

Table 10.3: euristic vs. Critical Level Policy an Aggregation Policy - Service Level

	Parameter Values					Critical Level Policy			euristic				Aggregation Policy		
	1	2	λ_1	λ_2	LT	S*	CL*	ETC*	S*	CL*	ETC*	% Gap	S*	ETC*	%Gap
BC	99%	90%	1.5	1.5	2	13	0	4.158	14	0	5.084	22.27%	17	8.010	92.63%
Vary 1	95%					13	0	4.158	13	0	4.158	0.00%	14	5.084	22.27%
	96%					13	0	4.158	14	0	5.084	22.27%	15	6.043	45.33%
	97%					13	0	4.158	14	0	5.084	22.27%	15	6.043	45.33%
	98%					13	0	4.158	14	0	5.084	22.27%	16	7.021	68.85%
	99%					13	0	4.158	14	0	5.084	22.27%	17	8.010	92.63%
Vary 2		70%				**12**	**2**	**3.703**	**12**	**0**	**3.282**	**-11.36%**	17	8.010	116.30%
		80%				13	0	4.158	13	0	4.158	0.00%	17	8.010	92.63%
		90%				13	0	4.158	14	0	5.084	22.27%	17	8.010	92.63%
		95%				14	0	5.084	15	0	6.043	18.85%	17	8.010	57.54%
Vary λ_1			0.5			9	0	3.161	10	0	4.077	28.98%	12	6.015	90.26%
			1			11	0	3.662	12	0	4.582	25.15%	15	7.508	105.04%
			1.5			13	0	4.158	14	0	5.084	22.27%	17	8.010	92.63%
			5			27	2	7.816	28	0	8.565	9.58%	30	10.523	34.62%
Vary λ_2				0.5		11	0	5.035	11	0	5.035	0.00%	12	6.015	19.46%
				1		12	0	4.582	12	0	4.582	0.00%	15	7.508	63.84%
				1.5		13	0	4.158	14	0	5.084	22.27%	17	8.010	92.63%
				5		25	0	5.759	26	0	6.668	15.78%	30	10.523	82.71%
Vary LT					1	9	0	3.161	10	0	4.077	28.98%	12	6.015	90.26%
					2	13	0	4.158	14	0	5.084	22.27%	17	8.010	92.63%
					3	17	0	5.145	18	0	6.082	18.21%	21	9.012	75.15%
					4	21	0	6.129	21	0	6.129	0.00%	25	10.013	63.36%

class, we found that the parameter constellation that just satisfies both α-service level constraints might not always be optimal. Instead, it might be beneficial to satisfy far more demands of class 2 customers than originally required. In particular, this is the case if the required α-service level for class 1 customers is very high and the α-service level for class 2 customers rather low. The approach we used and most of those results are transferable to the case of β-service level.

In our analysis, we focused on results that hold for arbitrary discrete demand distributions with a positive probability for zero demands. It seems that properties such as submodularity of the cost function allow more detailed results. This in turn requires special demand distributions. Therefore, it would be valuable to gain a deeper understanding on the relation between the demand distributions and the cost function.

10.4 Proofs

Proof of Proposition 17.

This is implied in Proposition 12. □

Proof of Proposition 18.

Equation (8.6) remains the same for all differences of S and CL. □

Proof of Proposition 19.

This is a special case of Proposition 13. □

Proof of Proposition 20.

Let (S, CL) satisfy the required α-service level for class 1 customers. By Proposition 19, $\Pr(B_1^{S,CL} = 0)$ is increasing in both, S and CL. Thus the first part of the proposition follows.

To prove the second part, we will give an example. Let demands be Poisson distributed with parameters $\lambda_1 = 1.25$ and $\lambda_2 = 1.75$. Let $LT = 2$. Then

$(9, 0)$ satisfies the α-service level constraint of $\alpha_1 \geq 99\%$ whereas $(8, 0)$ does not. However, $(8, 1)$ again satisfies the α-service level constraint. □

Proof of Proposition 21.

As an immediate consequence of Part 3 of Corollary 2, in particular the part concerning changes in CL, the optimal parameter constellation is amongst all parameter constellations $(S, 0)$ with $S \geq S_2^0$. By the same part of Corollary 2 and the statement concerning changes in S, the smallest S minimizes the cost function. □

Proof of Proposition 22.

By construction, either $S_2^0 > S_1^0$ and Proposition 21 applies, or all members of Ω fulfill both α-service level requirements and are thus potential minimizers of the objective function. Hence it remains to show that all other parameter constellations fulfilling the α-service level constraints imply the same or higher costs than those in the set Ω.

Clearly, for a given S, higher critical levels are sub-optimal, because the expected on-hand inventory at the end of a period is increasing in CL (Part 3 of Corollary 2). Since the expected on-hand inventory at the end of a period is increasing in S, solutions with a critical level of $CL = 0$ and a order-up-to level of $S > \max\{S_1^0, S_2^0\}$ cannot be optimal either. Similarly, all parameter constellations with a higher specific critical level CL and order-up-to levels S, S not likely, cannot be optimal. □

Proof of Proposition 23.

Let the required α-service level α_1 for class 1 customers be fixed. Let A_1 denote the following set: $A_1 := \{(S, CL_1^S) | S \leq S_1^0\}$. For arbitrary α_2, we additionally define the set $A_2(\alpha_2) := \{(S, CL) \mid \Pr(B_2^{S,CL} = 0) \geq \alpha_2\}$. Thus for arbitrary α_2, any potential optimizer has to be an element of $A_1 \cap A_2(\alpha_2)$.

In Figure 10.5 those sets are visualized for Poisson distributed demands with parameters $\lambda_1 = \lambda_2 = 1.5$, lead time $LT = 2$. and required α-service levels of $\alpha_1 \geq 99\%$ and $\alpha_2 \geq 96\%$. The further proof based on the fact that lowering α_2 the set $A_2(\alpha_2)$ grows "to the left" while the set A_1 remains the same. Thus more and more elements of A_1 become members of $A_2(\alpha_2)$ as well.

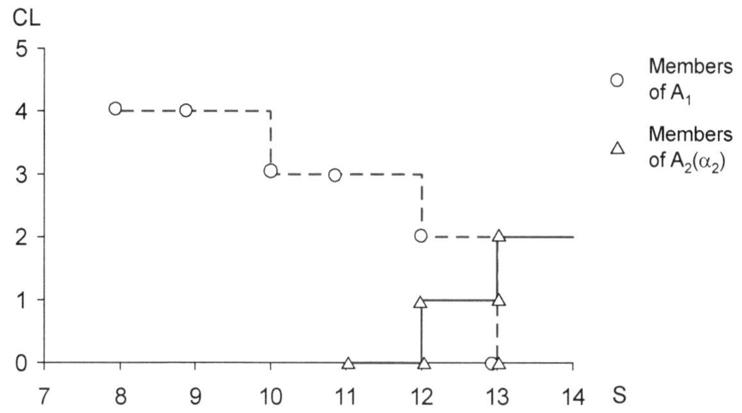

Figure 10.5: The sets A_1 and $A_2(\alpha_2)$

We will now provide a constructive argument to show the existence of the sequence of threshold service levels $st_i(\alpha_1)$ that fulfill the proposition: We define $st_0(\alpha_1) := \Pr(B_2^{S_0^1,0} = 0)$. For each $i \geq 1$, we define

$$\widetilde{S}_i := \max \quad \Big\{S|CL_1^S = i \text{ and } ETC^{S,i} < ETC^{S',CL_{S'}} \\ \text{for all } (S', CL_1^{S'}) \in A_1 \text{ with } CL_1^{S'} < i\Big\}$$

and

$$st_i(\alpha_1) = \begin{cases} \Pr(B_2^{\widetilde{S}_i,i} = 0) & \text{if } \widetilde{S}_i \text{ exists} \\ st_{i+1}(\alpha_1) & \text{else} \end{cases}$$

It should be noted that $\widetilde{S}_i > \widetilde{S}_{i+1}$ for all $i \geq 1$ because CL_S is non-increasing in S. Furthermore, note that this definition of the threshold service levels does not take into account that we originally required $\alpha_1 \geq \alpha_2$.

To show that those threshold service levels fulfill Proposition 23, let $\alpha_2 > \Pr(B_2^{S_1^0,0} = 0)$. Then $S_1^0 \leq S_2^0$ and by Proposition 21 $(S_2^0, 0)$ is optimal.

Next, assume that $\widetilde{S}_1$ exists and $\Pr(B_2^{S_1^0,0} = 0) \geq \alpha_2 > \Pr(B_2^{\widetilde{S}_1,1} = 0)$. Then the critical level of the optimal solution remains $CL = 0$, because $A_1 \cap A_2(\alpha_2) = (S_1^0, 0)$. If $\widetilde{S}_1$ does not exist, we consider $\Pr(B_2^{S_1^0,0} = 0) \geq \alpha_2 > \Pr(B_2^{\widetilde{S}_2,2} = 0)$ assuming $\widetilde{S}_2$ exists. In this case, $(S_1^0, 0)$ and thus $CL = 0$ remains optimal even if $A_1 \cap A_2(\alpha_2) = \{(S, CL_1^S) \in A_1 | CL_1^S \leq 1\}$.

We now assume that both $\widetilde{S}_1$ and $\widetilde{S}_2$ exist and $\Pr(B_2^{\widetilde{S}_1,1} = 0) \geq \alpha_2 > \Pr(B_2^{\widetilde{S}_2,2} = 0)$. Then $(\widetilde{S}_1, 1) \in A_1 \cap A_2\,(\alpha_2)$ and, by definition of $\widetilde{S}_1$, this parameter constellation is more cost-efficient than $(S_1^0, 0)$. Thus the critical level of the optimal solution rises to $CL = 1$. If there is $S' < \widetilde{S}_1$ with $(S', 1) \in A_1 \cap A_2\,(\alpha_2)$ then Corollary 2 implies $ETC^{S',1} \leq ETC^{\widetilde{S}_1,1}$. Thus those parameter constellations do not yield a rise in CL, but make sure that the optimal rationing level does not drop back to zero either. So the next rise, by definition of $\widetilde{S}_2$, occurs when $\Pr(B_2^{\widetilde{S}_2,2} = 0) \geq \alpha_2$ and so forth. □

Proof of Proposition 24.

To prove that the threshold service level $st_0(\alpha_1)$ is non-decreasing in α_1, it suffices to show the following property for a fixed required α-service level α_2 for class 2 customers: If $(S_2^0, 0)$ is optimal for α_1, then $(S_2^0, 0)$ is optimal for any $\overline{\alpha}_1$ with $\overline{\alpha}_1 \leq \alpha_1$. Then the claim follows by the definition of $st_0(\alpha_1)$ as $\Pr(B_2^{S_1^0,0} = 0)$.

Let S_1^0 and $\overline{S_1^0}$ denote the minimal order-up-to levels such that $\Pr(B_1^{S_1^0,0} = 0) \geq \alpha_1$ and $\Pr(B_1^{\overline{S_1^0},0} = 0) \geq \overline{\alpha}_1$ respectively. By Proposition 10.3, $S_1^0 \geq \overline{S_1^0}$. If $(S_2^0, 0)$ is optimal for α_1, then $S_2^0 \geq S_1^0$ and therefore also $S_2^0 \geq \overline{S_1^0}$. This in turn implies that $(S_2^0, 0)$ is optimal for $\overline{\alpha}_1$ as well. □

Proof of Proposition 25.

We will again provide a constructive argument to show the existence of the sequence of threshold service levels $st_i'(\alpha_1)$ that fulfill the proposition: We define $st_0'(\alpha_1) = \Pr(B_2^{S_1^0,0} = 0)$. For each $i \geq 1$, we define

$$st_i'(\alpha_1) = \begin{cases} \Pr(B_2^{S_1^0-i,CL_1^{S_1^0-i}} = 0) & \text{if } ETC^{S_1^0-i,CL_1^{S_1^0-i}} < ETC^{S_1^0-j,CL_1^{S_1^0-j}} \\ & \text{for all } j < i \\ st_{i+1}'(\alpha_1) & \text{else} \end{cases}$$

Note that this definition just adds additional threshold service levels to those defined in Proposition 23. The proof is then completely analogous to the proof of Proposition 23. □

Proof of Proposition 26.

To show that the cost function is increasing in α_2 for fixed α_1, we will make use of the threshold service levels defined in Propositions 23 and 25. By definition of both kinds of threshold service levels, we have the following relation $\{st_i(\alpha_1)\}_i \subseteq \{st'_j(\alpha_1)\}_j$. Thus we may concentrate on the threshold service levels $st'_j(\alpha_1)$ only. Now - again by definition of the threshold service levels - if α_2 drops below the threshold service level a cost decrease is incurred. Inbetween two threshold levels, however, the costs remain constant. This proves the proposition for all $\alpha_2 \leq st'_0(\alpha_1)$.

For $\alpha_2 > st'_0(\alpha_1)$ the cost function is increasing in α_2 for fixed α_1 because of Proposition 17 and Corollary 2: In this situation, the optimizer is $(S_2^0, 0)$. By Proposition 17 increasing α_2 might require increasing S_2^0. This in turn leads to higher costs (Corollary 2). The cost function is also a step function because costs do not increase continuously, but only if the increase in α_2 requires increasing S_2^0. □

Proof of Proposition 27.

These properties follow immediately from Propositions 12 and 13 □

Proof of Proposition 28.

As before, let (S, CL) satisfy the required fill rate probability for class 1 customers. By Proposition 27, the class 1 fill rate $1 - \frac{EB_1^{S,CL}}{ED_1}$ is increasing in both, S and CL. Thus the first part of the proposition follows.

To prove the second part, we will again give an example. Let demands be Poisson distributed with parameters $\lambda_1 = 1.25$ and $\lambda_2 = 1.75$. Let $LT = 2$ and $\beta_1 = 93\%$. Then $(9, 0)$ satisfies the fill rate constraint with 93.8% whereas $(8, 0)$ with a fill rate of 90.8% does not. However, $(8, 1)$ satisfies the fill rate constraint (95.4%). □

Proof of Proposition 29.

To prove that S_2^{Low} is a lower limit for S_2^0, we show that the probability $F_{D^{LT+1}}(S - CL) + \overline{F_{D^{LT}} * f_1}(S - CL)\ f_2(0)$ exceeds $\Pr(B_2^{S,CL} = 0)$. Thus the same parameter constellation leads to a higher α-service level and hence the required α-service level for class 2 customers α_2 might then already be met by a smaller difference of S and CL. Therefore, we have $S_2^{Low} \leq S_2^0$. Note that for two density functions f and g the c.d.f. of $f * g$ equals $F * g$. Thus we have

$$\begin{aligned} & F_{D^{LT+1}}(S - CL) + \overline{F_{D^{LT}} * f_1}(S - CL)\ f_2(0) \\ = \; & \Pr(S - IO - D_1 - D_2 \geq CL) + \Pr(S - IO - D_1 < CL) \Pr(D_2 = 0) \qquad (10.7) \end{aligned}$$

The first part, i.e., $F_{D^{LT+1}}(S - CL) = \Pr(S - IO - D_1 - D_2 \geq CL)$, coincides with the first summand of Equation (10.2). The second part of Equation (10.2) explicitly expressing the stochastic dependence between class 2 backorders and inventory on order reads as

$$\begin{aligned} & \Pr(S - IO - D_1 < CL, D_2 = 0, B_2 = 0) \\ = \; & \sum_{io=0}^{\infty} \sum_{d_1=S-io-CL+1}^{\infty} \Pr(D_1 = d_1) \Pr(D_2 = 0) \Pr(B_2 = 0, IO = io) \end{aligned}$$

$$\begin{aligned} = \; & \sum_{io=0}^{\infty} \sum_{d_1=S-io-CL+1}^{\infty} \Pr(D_1 = d_1) \Pr(D_2 = 0) \Pr(IO = io) \\ & \Pr(B_2 = 0 | IO = io) \end{aligned}$$

Clearly, this is smaller than

$$\begin{aligned} & \sum_{io=0}^{\infty} \sum_{d_1=S-io-CL+1}^{\infty} \Pr(D_1 = d_1) \Pr(D_2 = 0) \Pr(IO = io) \\ = \; & \Pr(S - IO - D_1 < CL) \Pr(D_2 = 0) \end{aligned}$$

Thus Equation (10.7) is indeed an overestimate for the probability of zero backorders of class 2. □

Chapter 11

Dynamic Rationing Policies

It is known or assumed that the optimal rationing policy has state-dependent critical levels (e.g. Gayon et al. (2005), Frank et al. (2003)). However, under periodic review now complete characterization of such an optimal policy is available. In this chapter we address this issue and suggest two state-dependent rationing policies for periodic review settings that take into account the backorder clearing. Although these rationing policies are not optimal, they represent an improvement over the constant rationing policy and are still easy to implement. We will see that under cost-optimal backorder clearing there are situations in which the constant rationing policy performs almost as well as the best of the two dynamic rationing policies and the increased complexity may not be worth it.

We again assume that the two demand classes are prioritized based on penalty costs with $p_1 \geq p_2$. Our objective is to study the benefits of dynamic rationing policies compared to the constant rationing policy w.r.t. to the expected total cost per period,

$$ETC = h\ EIH + p_1\ EB_1 + p_2\ EB_2. \tag{11.1}$$

In the next two sections, we introduce the two dynamic rationing policies,

K. Möllering, *Inventory Rationing*, Edition KWV,
https://doi.org/10.1007/978-3-658-24255-8_11

the next period optimization policy (Section 11.1) and the linear critical level policy (Section 11.2). In Section 11.3, we will compare these policies to the constant rationing policy (CRP) of Chapter 9. We conclude in Section 11.4. For proofs, the reader is referred to Section 11.5.

We will evaluate the performance of these policies based on simulation. Obeying by the sequence of events outlined in Section 8.1, the critical level for a period is determined after class 1 backorders and new demand have been dealt with.

11.1 The Next Period Optimization Policy

11.1.1 The Policy

Under positive lead time we must have detailed information on the inventory on order to make optimal rationing decisions. Thus it is intuitive to include all periods in the decision that we have information about. Unfortunately, determining a rationing level by optimizing the next LT periods quickly becomes very complex. On the other hand, it is intuitive that periods are more important the closer to the present they are. Thus, the first dynamic rationing rule we are going to analyze optimizes the sum of current period's class 2 penalty and inventory holding costs and expected class 1 penalty cost of the upcoming period. We call the resulting policy "Next Period Optimization" (NPO) and determine the optimal rationing level CL_t^{NPO} as the cl minimizing

$$p_2\ b_{2t}(cl) +\ h\ ih_t(cl) +\ p_1\ EB_{1t+1}(cl). \qquad (11.2)$$

We apply simulation to study the impact of this dynamic rationing rule. In each period, we generate a random demand for each customer class. Based on the state of the system at the beginning of each period, we clear class 1 backorders and fill new class 1 demands. The inventory after serving class 1, i_t^I, is then given by $i_t^I = \max\{0, i_t - b_{1t-1} - d_{1t}\}$. If $i_t^I = 0$, then there is no inventory left to serve class 2 customers and all new class 2 demands are backordered. If $i_t^I > 0$, then we determine the optimal rationing level CL_t^{NPO} assuming $i_t^I - b_{2t-1} - d_{2t} \leq CL_t^{NPO} \leq i_t^I$. Rationing levels exceeding

i_t^I affect the system in the same way as $CL_t^{NPO} = i_t^I$. Rationing levels smaller than $i_t^I - b_{2t-1} - d_{2t}$ do not lead to lower class 2 backorders and inventory at the end of period t, because there is no additional demand of class 2 customers. Proposition 30 gives a simple formula for calculating the optimal critical level under NPO.

Proposition 30 *In each period t, the optimal rationing level under NPO, CL_t^{NPO}, is the smallest cl with $i_t^I - b_{2t-1} - d_{2t} \leq cl \leq i_t^I$ such that*

$$\sum_{j=cl+d_{t-LT}+1}^{\infty} \Pr(D_{1t+1} = j) \leq \frac{h + p_2}{p_1}. \tag{11.3}$$

As an immediate consequence of this result, the optimal rationing level CL_t^{NPO} is increasing in class 1 penalty cost p_1 and decreasing in class 2 penalty cost p_2 and holding cost h.

Note that inventory for class 1 customers is never rationed. Nevertheless, class 1 backorders in the subsequent period $t+1$ depend on the rationing level specified in period t via the inventory left over at the end of period t.

11.1.2 Structural results

The way NPO works differs significantly from CRP. For instance, the average rationing level is far higher. Figure 11.1 shows the rationing level distribution for the case of Poisson demands with parameters $\lambda_1 = \lambda_2 = 1.5$, lead time $LT = 2$, order-up-to level $S = 15$, penalty costs $p_1 = 1000$ and $p_2 = 10$, and holding cost $h = 1$. In this situation, the optimal rationing level under CRP is $CL^{CRP} = 1$. The optimal rationing level under NPO, CL_t^{NPO}, however, will be as high as possible to provide maximum security for class 1 customers in the upcoming period. It also takes into account the demand of class 2 customers in the actual period t. If this demand is low there is no need to lower the rationing level further. This intuition is also supported by the fact that under this policy, the expectation of the rationing level and the expected inventory on hand at the end of a period coincide (see proof of Proposition 30 for details).

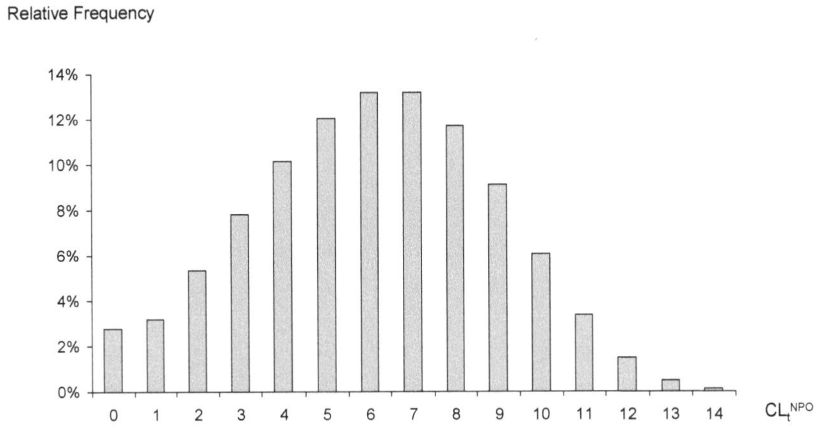

Figure 11.1: Distribution of the rationing level CL_t^{NPO}

11.2 The Linear Critical Level Policy

11.2.1 The Policy

While NPO only focuses on the effect of the rationing decision for the upcoming period $t+1$, the linear critical level policy (LCL) takes into account the incoming orders of the next LT periods. These are weighted by a factor $\frac{\nu}{i+1}$ with $i = 0$ corresponding to the next incoming order, i.e., to the demand observed LT periods earlier, d_{t-LT}. This way, the highest weight is put on orders arriving in the next period. We refer to ν as the weight factor, $\nu \in \mathbb{R}_+$. To determine the rationing level CL_t^{LCL}, the sum of the weighted incoming orders is subtracted from a constant κ and the result rounded to the next integer, i.e.,

$$CL_t^{LCL} = \left\lceil \kappa - \sum_{i=0}^{LT-1} \frac{\nu}{i+1} d_{t-LT+i} \right\rceil . \tag{11.4}$$

A rationing level slightly above a certain integer indicates that the integer itself would not be sufficient. Therefore, we round to the next higher integer. Due to integer-valued demands, the results then coincide with those we would obtain if we allowed for non-integer rationing levels and did not round at all.

Experiments underline that this is superior to rounding to the nearest integer or cutting off decimal digits. For each combination of demand distributions, lead time and cost structure, optimal values for the constant κ and the weight factor ν can be found.

As for NPO, we apply simulation to study the impact of the linear critical level policy. The rationing level is again determined after class 1 has been served. At this point of time, the order that will be issued at the end of this period t is known because demands have already been observed. Thus we may determine the rationing level based on Equation (11.4). The optimal values for κ and ν can be determined by simulation and exhaustive search.

In view of Equation (11.4), exponentially decreasing weights ν^{i+1} known from forecasting with single exponential smoothing also seem to be reasonable. However, experiments indicate that our linear model outperforms such a policy. Under exponentially decreasing weights, the emphasis on incoming orders in the next LT periods decreases stronger than under linearly decreasing weights. It seems that linearly decreasing weights thus lead to a better mix of information included in the final rationing level. Figure 11.2 compares the savings of these two policies over CRP for a situation with Poisson demands with parameters $\lambda_1 = \lambda_2 = 1.5$, penalty costs $p_1 = 100$ and $p_2 = 10$, and holding cost $h = 1$.

If the lead time is one period only, then there is a one-to-one correspondence between the one and the other rationing policy. Thus there is no difference in savings. The percentage of savings first decreases, before it increases again. This effect is caused by optimizing parameters averaging over more than one period. We will explore this in more detail in Section 11.3.2.

11.2.2 Structural results

The general rationale behind the way LCL sets the rationing level, is similar to the rationing level determination under NPO. Figure 11.3 shows the rationing level distribution for the case of Poisson demands with parameters $\lambda_1 = \lambda_2 = 1.5$, lead time $LT = 2$, order-up-to level $S = 16$, constant $\kappa = 6.1$, weight factor $\nu = 0.8$, penalty costs $p_1 = 1000$ and $p_2 = 10$ and holding cost $h = 1$. Again, the average rationing level under LCL is usually higher than

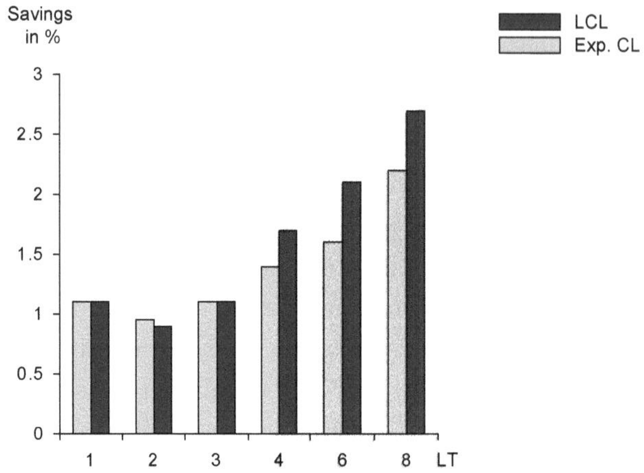

Figure 11.2: Savings under LCL and a policy with exponential critical level compared to CRP

under CRP (in the example, $CL^{CRP} = 1$). However, under LCL the rationing level cannot exceed the constant κ. By Equation (11.4), the mean of the rationing level CL_t^{LCL} is approximately $\left\lceil \kappa - \sum_{i=0}^{LT-1} \frac{\nu}{i+1} LT \cdot ED \right\rceil$. It is thus not as high as the expected rationing level under NPO, CL^{NPO}. This role inbetween CRP and NPO is also true in other respects: In contrast to NPO, LCL does not react to current class 2 demand, but averages future replenishments. Under CRP, we search for the parameters optimizing the average expected cost of (infinitely many) periods.

The average rationing level increases with lead time, but this increase is moderate compared to the increase in the order-up-to level S. In the setting above, using a lead time of $LT = 10$ instead of 2, the order-up-to level S^{LCL} increases from 16 to 44, whereas the expected rationing level CL^{LCL} increases from 3.08 to 4.38. Thus the rationing level in a way secures a safety stock for upcoming class 1 demand taking into account that variability of demand and inventory on order is increasing in the lead time.

Two parameters determine the dynamics of the rationing level CL_t^{LCL}: The constant κ and the weight factor ν. While the cost function is rather insensitive in κ, slight differences in ν yield significant differences in the expected

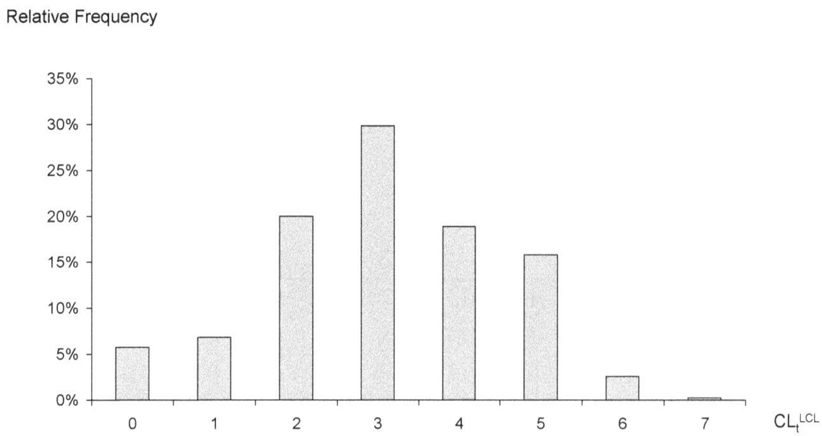

Figure 11.3: Distribution of the rationing level CL_t^{LCL}

total cost. Table 11.1 underlines those findings for Poisson demands with parameters $\lambda_1 = \lambda_2 = 1.5$, lead time $LT = 2$, order-up-to level $S = 16$, penalty costs $p_1 = 1000$ and $p_2 = 10$ and holding cost $h = 1$ based on 25 replications of 8 million periods.

		ν		
		0.7	0.8	0.9
	5.6	7.979	8.078	8.195
κ	5.7	7.976	8.027	8.180
	5.8	7.983	8.031	8.163

Table 11.1: Sensitivity of the total cost per period under LCL

If we explicitly consider standard deviation (0.010 - 0.016 in this case), we cannot really conclude whether $\kappa = 5.6$ is superior to $\kappa = 5.7$. In view of Equation (11.4), this result - due to rounding and the integrality of demand - is not surprising. It implies, that the same expected cost can be attributed to more than one parameter combination.

The last structural property worth mentioning concerns situations with lead time $LT = 1$ as opposed to those with lead time $LT > 1$. For $LT = 1$, the weight factor ν is notably higher than for longer lead times when it is rather stable amongst settings in which only the lead time is varied. This behavior is indicated in Table 11.2 for Poisson demands with parameters $\lambda_1 = \lambda_2 = 1.5$, class 2 penalty cost $p_2 = 10$ and holding cost $h = 1$.

		LT						
		1	2	3	4	6	8	10
	100	1.1	0.7	0.7	0.7	0.8	0.8	0.8
p_1	1000	1.1	0.7	0.8	0.8	0.8	0.8	0.8
	10000	0.9	0.7	0.8	0.8	0.8	0.9	0.9

Table 11.2: Optimal weight factors for different class 1 penalty costs and lead times

For $LT = 1$, only one integer-valued order is subtracted from the constant κ. Therefore, the weight factor does not have to trade-off the influence of several future replenishments, but can explicitly reflect all available information. The influence of averaging several future periods will become more obvious when we compare LCL to CRP in the next section.

11.3 Efficiency of the Dynamic Rationing Policies

In this section, we evaluate the dynamic rationing policies introduced in the preceding sections. For Poisson demands, we benchmark these policies against the constant rationing policy and interpret the differences. Finally, we compare the two dynamic rationing policies with each other.

Note that the results for the dynamic rationing policies are simulation-based and therefore vary slightly with each replication. We are aware of this variability, although we will mainly present results that are based on the means and do not explicitly consider the standard deviation.

11.3.1 Next Period Optimization and Constant Rationing Policy

NPO works with a far higher rationing level. This leads to similar structural results as stated for critical level variation under CRP in Corollary 2. These effects are stated in Proposition 31.

Proposition 31 *For a fixed order-up-to level S and assuming a rationing level of $CL^{CRP} = 0$, the following properties hold:*

1. *Expected class 1 backorders are lower under NPO than under CRP, i.e., $EB_1^{NPO} \leq EB_1^{CRP}$.*
2. *Expected class 2 backorders are lower under NPO than under CRP, i.e., $EB_2^{NPO} \geq EB_2^{CRP}$.*
3. *Expected inventory on hold at the end of a period is higher under NPO than under CRP, i.e., $EIH^{NPO} \geq EIH^{CRP}$.*

It is worth noting, that those relations are no longer true in general if $CL^{CRP} \neq 0$. Furthermore, this result does not shed any insight into cost and savings under NPO.

Considering expected total cost and savings per period, we also obtain very structural improvements (see Table 11.3): The cost savings increase in the holding cost. The higher the class 1 demand rate the higher the performance increase. The same holds for class 1 penalty costs. In general, class 2 penalty cost and the class 2 demand rate both work in opposite directions. A special case occurs if the difference between class 1 and class 2 penalty costs is low or even zero. NPO does not see the difference in penalty costs and still rations inventory in favor of class 1 demand. This leads to higher backorders than necessary. Therefore, in these situations, NPO is outperformed by CRP. Table A.1 indicates an exception in the structured changes for a very low demand rate for class 2 customers. In such a situation, there is hardly any demand to ration at all and therefore hardly any situation in which CL^{NPO} differs from CL^{CRP}.

The observed behavior is intuitive: In reaction to high holding cost, CRP favours a low rationing level. Then, more inventory is used to fill customer

Table 11.3 - e t Perio ptimi ation Policy vs. Constant ationing Policy

	Parameter Values						C P			P				
	h	p_1	p_2	λ_1	λ_2	LT	$S^{C\ P}$	$CL^{C\ P}$	$ETC^{C\ P}$	$S^{\ P}$	$ETC^{\ P}$	^{P}	%Gap	Abs. Gap
BC	1	100	10	1	1	1	8	0	4.651	8	4.621	0.003	0.64%	0.030
Vary h	0.01						12	0	0.085	12	0.085	0.000	0.05%	0.000
	0.1						10	0	0.666	10	0.664	0.001	0.30%	0.002
	1						8	0	4.651	8	4.621	0.003	0.64%	0.030
	10						5	0	23.299	5	22.799	0.011	2.15%	0.500
Vary p_1		10					7	0	3.932	7	3.932	0.003	0.01%	0.000
		100					8	0	4.651	8	4.621	0.003	0.64%	0.030
		1000					9	1	6.028	9	5.645	0.006	6.35%	0.383
		10000					11	1	7.577	**10**	**6.765**	**0.014**	**10.72%**	**0.812**
Vary p_2			1				7	1	3.951	7	3.684	0.002	6.74%	0.266
			5				7	0	4.380	7	4.166	0.003	4.89%	0.214
			10				8	0	4.651	8	4.621	0.003	0.64%	0.030
			50				9	0	5.673	9	5.677	0.005	-0.06%	-0.004
			100				9	0	6.239	9	6.248	0.013	-0.15%	-0.009
Vary λ_1				0.1			4	0	3.089	4	3.088	0.003	0.02%	0.001
				0.5			6	0	3.783	6	3.759	0.004	0.65%	0.025
				1			8	0	4.651	8	4.621	0.003	0.64%	0.030
				5			19	0	8.864	19	8.712	0.009	1.72%	0.152
Vary λ_2					0.1		6	0	4.569	6	4.547	0.005	0.48%	0.022
					0.5		7	0	4.584	7	4.546	0.004	0.81%	0.037
					1		8	0	4.651	8	4.621	0.003	0.64%	0.030
					5		17	0	6.602	17	6.598	0.006	0.06%	0.004
Vary LT						1	8	0	4.651	8	4.621	0.003	0.64%	0.030
						2	10	0	5.705	10	5.545	0.006	2.80%	0.160
						3	13	0	6.611	13	6.330	0.004	4.25%	0.281
						4	16	0	7.243	15	7.093	0.013	2.07%	0.150

demands. As the rationing level is constant, there is no possibility to keep inventory if the current inventory is very low and the next replenishment is not high either. NPO keeps this ability to react to those variabilities and reduces cost. Under CRP, a higher class 1 demand rate leads to higher class 1 backorders. Under NPO, we may react to peak backorders of class 1 by increasing the rationing level. Thus class 1 backorders under NPO increase less strong. Additionally, we may lower the rationing level to avoid class 2 backorders if the likelihood of class 1 backorders in the upcoming period is low. This is particularly advantageous compared to CRP if $CL^{CRP} > 0$. Both means lead to a cost reductions. To illustrate these explanations, Table 11.4 lists the backorder and inventory for different penalty costs under both, CRP and NPO, assuming Poisson demands with parameter $\lambda_1 = \lambda_2 = 1$, lead time $LT = 1$, and holdings cost $h = 1$. In all cases, the optimal solutions are compared.

		CRP			*NPO*		
p_1	p_2	EB_1	EB_2	EIH	EB_1	EB_2	EIH
100	1	0.006	0.171	3.177	0.004	0.121	3.125
100	5	0.009	0.076	3.085	0.004	0.121	3.125
100	10	0.003	0.030	4.034	0.003	0.033	4.035
1000	10	0.001	0.030	5.031	0.000	0.029	5.030
10000	10	0.000	0.004	7.004	0.000	0.024	6.024

Table 11.4: Expected backorders and inventory at the end of a period under CRP and NPO

If the class 1 demand rate increases, peak class 1 backorders become more frequent and higher. Thus the dynamic rationing policy is increasingly valuable. For high class 1 penalty cost, cost savings are also due to reduced class 2 backorders because in those cases $CL^{CRP} > 0$. Furthermore, the flexibility enables the system to run with lower inventory. The higher the class 2 demand rate, the more class 2 demands are affected by occasionally higher rationing levels and thus backordered. If class 2 penalty cost increases, then the additional class 2 backorders are more expensive which explains the decrease of the performance gap in class 2 penalty cost.

A priori, there is no reason why this behavior should not hold for arbitrary lead times. However, Table 11.3 indicates that savings increase up to a certain lead time and decrease if the lead time is prolonged even further. Thus there seems to be an optimal lead time for this policy. Additionally varying the cost structure, we find that this optimal lead time is lower, the higher class 1 penalty cost. Figure 11.4 shows the development of the cost savings for a setting with Poisson demands with demand rates $\lambda_1 = \lambda_2 = 1.5$, class 2 penalty cost $p_2 = 10$, and holding cost $h = 1$. While it is intuitive

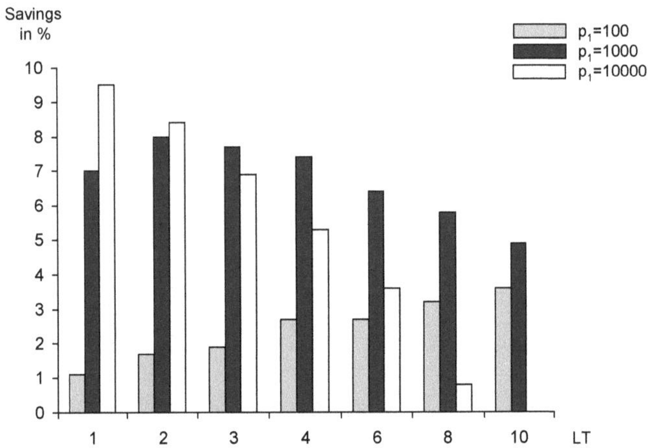

Figure 11.4: Savings of NPO compared to CRP for different class 1 penalty costs

that savings will not increase forever, the fact that the percentage of savings achieved is not always ordered in line with class 1 penalty costs is at a first glance surprising. Then again, NPO will not buffer inventory for more than one period in advance. Occasionally, this leads to high class 1 penalty cost because in earlier periods too much inventory has been used for class 2 demands. The higher class 1 penalty cost the more this policy suffers from this suboptimality. This deficiency may even lead to CRP outperforming NPO for long lead times.

For these reasons, we assume that this structural behavior holds for general demand distributions and state this in Claim 1.

Claim 1 *For the performance gap between the policy "Nest Period Optimization" (NPO) and the CRP, the following properties hold for low lead times:*

1. *The higher the class 1 demand rate* λ_1, *the higher* $ETC^{CRP} - ETC^{NPO}$.
2. *Except for very low demand rates, the higher the class 2 demand rate* λ_2, *the lower* $ETC^{CRP} - ETC^{NPO}$.
3. *The higher the class 1 penalty cost* p_1, *the higher* $ETC^{CRP} - ETC^{NPO}$.
4. *The higher the class 2 penalty cost* p_2, *the lower* $ETC^{CRP} - ETC^{NPO}$.

11.3.2 Linear Critical Level Policy and Constant Rationing Policy

First, it is worth noting that LCL can be viewed as an extension of CRP: Setting the order-up-to level $S^{LCL} = S^{CRP}$, the constant $\kappa = CL^{CRP}$, and the weight factor $\nu = 0$, we obtain $ETC^{LCL} = ETC^{CRP}$. Thus CRP will never outperform LCL - as opposed to NPO.

LCL affects the cost drivers backorders and inventory in the same way as NPO. Thus results analogous to Proposition 31 hold. These are summarized in Proposition 32.

Proposition 32 *For a fixed order-up-to level* S *and assuming a rationing level of* $CL^{CRP} = 0$, *the following properties hold:*

1. *Expected class 1 backorders are lower under LCL than under CRP, i.e.,* $EB_1^{LCL} \leq EB_1^{CRP}$.
2. *Expected class 2 backorders are lower under LCL than under CRP, i.e.,* $EB_2^{LCL} \geq EB_2^{CRP}$.
3. *Expected inventory on hold at the end of a period is higher under LCL than under CRP, i.e.,* $EIH^{LCL} \geq EIH^{CRP}$.

Again, bare in mind, that those relations are not necessarily true if $CL^{CRP} \neq 0$.

Considering savings in expected total cost, we again observe structured results (see Table 11.5). Savings are increasing in holding cost h and class 1 penalty cost p_1 and increasing the higher the class 1 demand rate λ_1. They are decreasing in class 2 penalty cost p_2 and in the class 2 demand parameter λ_2 (again with the exception of very low class 2 demand rates). The development of both, the constant κ and the weight factor ν also follow regular patterns.

These structures are due to the same reasons as before and there is no immediate reason why these findings should not extent to other demand distributions. Thus we assume that the structure of savings can be observed for any demand distributions as stated in Claim 2.

Claim 2 *For the performance gap between the policy "Linear Critical Level" (LCL) and the CRP, the following properties hold:*

1. *The higher the class 1 demand rate λ_1, the higher $ETC^{CRP} - ETC^{LCL}$.*
2. *Except for very low demand rates, the higher the class 2 demand rate λ_2, the lower $ETC^{CRP} - ETC^{LCL}$.*
3. *The higher the class 1 penalty cost p_1, the higher $ETC^{CRP} - ETC^{LCL}$.*
4. *The higher the class 2 penalty cost p_2, the lower $ETC^{CRP} - ETC^{LCL}$.*

As already mentioned, the behavior of LCL for lead time $LT = 1$ differs from that for longer lead times. As a consequence, savings compared to CRP peak in $LT = 1$ and then drop to a lower level. For lead times greater than one, a pattern similar to that under NPO can be observed with increased savings to a certain optimal lead time and decreased savings thereafter. Figure 11.5 visualizes this pattern for a setting with demand rates $\lambda_1 = \lambda_2 = 1.5$, class 2 penalty cost $p_2 = 10$ and holding cost $h = 1$ (same setting as Figure 11.4).

Again, optimal lead times decrease in class 1 penalty cost. For very high class 1 penalty cost, we observe a kind of stationarity. However, tests with

Table 11.5 - Linear Critical Level Policy vs. Constant ationing Policy

	Parameter Values						C P			LCL						
	h	p_1	p_2	λ_1	λ_2	LT	$S^{C\ P}$	$CL^{C\ P}$	$ETC^{C\ P}$	S^{LCL}			ETC^{LCL}	LCL	%Gap	Abs.Gap
BC	1	100	10	1	1	1	8	0	4.651	8	1.7	1	4.618	0.003	0.71%	0.033
Vary h	0.01						12	0	0.085	12	2.2	1.1	0.085	0.000	0.22%	0.000
	0.1						10	0	0.666	10	1.8	1.1	0.663	0.001	0.39%	0.003
	1						8	0	4.651	8	1.7	1.0	4.618	0.003	0.71%	0.033
	10						5	0	23.299	5	1.5	1.0	22.779	0.009	2.23%	0.520
Vary p_1		10					7	0	3.932	7	0	0	3.932	0.001	0.01%	0.000
		100					8	0	4.651	8	1.7	1.0	4.618	0.003	0.71%	0.033
		1000					9	1	6.028	9	3.6	1.1	5.635	0.006	6.52%	0.393
		10000					11	1	7.577	**10**	**4.9**	**1.2**	**6.751**	**0.021**	**10.90%**	**0.826**
Vary p_2			1				7	1	3.951	7	2.8	1.3	3.683	0.002	6.78%	0.268
			5				7	0	4.380	7	2.6	1.1	4.165	0.002	4.92%	0.216
			10				8	0	4.651	8	1.7	1.0	4.618	0.003	0.71%	0.033
			50				9	0	5.673	9	0.9	0.9	5.672	0.006	0.02%	0.001
			100				9	0	6.239	9	0	0	6.239	0.001	0.00%	0.000
Vary λ_1				0.1			4	0	3.089	4	0	0	3.088	0.001	0.03%	0.001
				0.5			6	0	3.783	6	0.7	1.0	3.757	0.001	0.70%	0.027
				1			8	0	4.651	8	1.7	1.0	4.618	0.003	0.71%	0.033
				5			19	0	8.864	19	6.3	0.8	8.712	0.009	1.72%	0.152
Vary λ_2					0.1		6	0	4.569	6	2	1.1	4.544	0.003	0.55%	0.025
					0.5		7	0	4.584	7	1.8	1	4.544	0.003	0.86%	0.039
					1		8	0	4.651	8	1.7	1.0	4.618	0.003	0.71%	0.033
					5		17	0	6.602	17	4.7	2.6	6.597	0.003	0.08%	0.005
Vary LT						1	8	0	4.651	8	1.7	1.0	4.618	0.003	0.71%	0.033
						2	10	0	5.705	10	2.9	0.8	5.598	0.004	1.88%	0.107
						3	13	0	6.611	13	3.5	0.7	6.374	0.004	3.59%	0.237
						4	16	0	7.243	15	4.2	0.7	7.129	0.001	1.57%	0.114

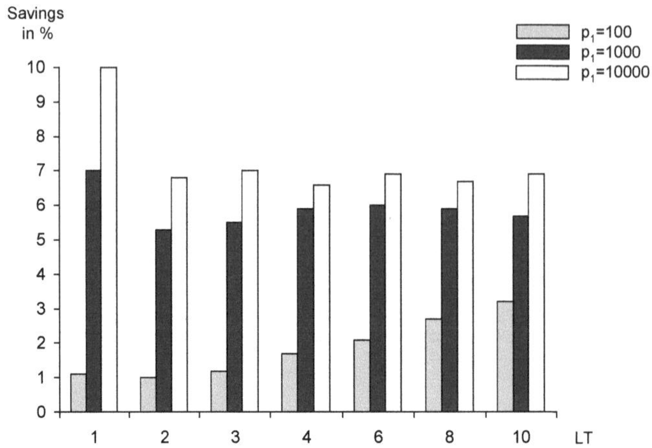

Figure 11.5: Savings of LCL compared to CRP for different class 1 penalty costs

longer lead times also show a decrease, e.g. for $LT = 16$ the cost savings drop to 4.7%. Therefore, we assume that in such a case, the decrease is very slow and the seemingly stationary cost savings result from the integer-valued parameters under CRP. In contrast to NPO, savings of LCL compared to CRP always seem to be higher the higher class 1 penalty cost. LCL is future-oriented and adjusts to different penalty costs via the weight factor ν. Hence, the explanation for the different behavior under NPO does not carry over to LCL.

11.3.3 Next Period Optimization and Linear Critical Level Policy

We have seen that the rationing level under NPO and LCL are distributed similarly, typically with expected rationing levels $CL^{NPO} \geq CL^{LCL}$. Furthermore, both policies share the phenomenon of an "optimal" lead time. This leads to similar saving patterns over CRP. In this section, we compare the benefits of NPO and LCL. We define the difference in savings by

$$\Delta = \frac{ETC^{LCL} - ETC^{NPO}}{ETC^{CRP}}.$$

Thus positive values of Δ indicate that LCL outperforms NPO whereas Δ is negative if NPO is superior to LCL. Comparing Tables 11.3 and 11.5, the two dynamic rationing policies seem to differ only very slightly. However, this is not true for other demand distributions. Figure 11.6 displays the development of the difference in savings for a setting with Poisson demands with parameters $\lambda_1 = \lambda_2 = 1.5$, class 2 penalty cost $p_2 = 10$ and holding cost $h = 1$. Due to best fitting possibilities, differences are low for lead

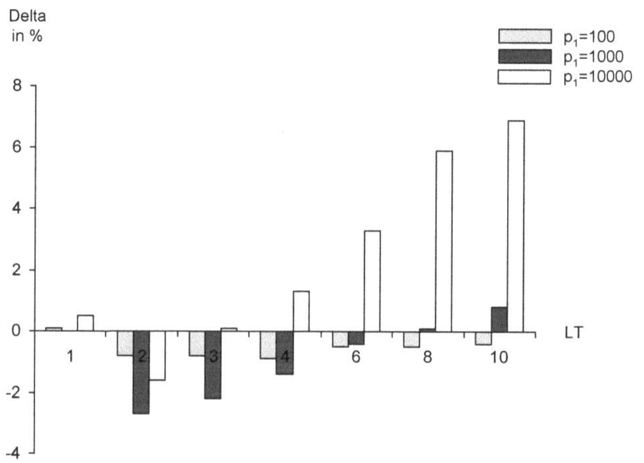

Figure 11.6: Difference between savings under LCL and NPO for different class 1 penalty costs

time $LT = 1$. For other lower lead times, NPO achieves higher savings than LCL because LCL has to average the weight factor ν (see discussion in the preceding section). However, the longer the lead time, the better LCL. This holds in particular, if additionally class 1 penalty cost is high. We already looked at the sharp decrease in savings under NPO for high class 1 penalty cost and saw that LCL behaves differently, which explains this result.

We so far focused our examples on different class 1 penalty costs. In fact, not the penalty cost alone but a combination of the class 1 demand rate and class 1 penalty cost as opposed to the class 2 demand rate and class 2 penalty cost are driving the cost savings. This can easily be seen for NPO: A high class 1 penalty cost and a low class 1 demand rates lead to the same decision rule as a high class 1 demand rate and a low class 1 penalty cost. For LCL, this is not as obvious as these relations are taken into account in the weight factor ν but experiments indicate a similar finding.

If we look at the total amount of savings achieved under the dynamic rationing policies, we may additionally conclude that neither of the two dynamic rationing rules achieved significant savings for low difference in penalty costs. Baring in mind that rationing increases complexity of the system it might be wise in such situations to stick to a non-rationing system.

11.4 Conclusion

In this chapter, we have suggested two dynamic rationing policies. With these policies we address the issue that little is known about dynamic rationing levels in a periodic review system that take into account the backorder clearing mechanism. The two policies allow for substantial savings over a constant rationing policy if the difference in either demand rates or penalty costs is high. There is little difference between the performance of both policies for a lead time of one period. While NPO performs better for other low lead times, LCL fully develops its potential for longer lead times. However, both policies share the phenomenon of the optimal lead time. Thus it seems reasonable that for very long lead times, LCL cannot keep its advantage over CRP to such an extent that it is worth the increased complexity. This leads to the recommendation as displayed in Figure 11.7 for various differences in penalty costs.

The findings underline the intuition that a dynamic rationing rule should put more emphasis on the near future than on the far future. Another factor that could directly influence a state-dependent critical level are the existing backorders of the low priority customers. High amounts of class 2 backorders could lead to a lower rationing level because the cost associated with them might be worth the higher risk of future class 1 backorders.

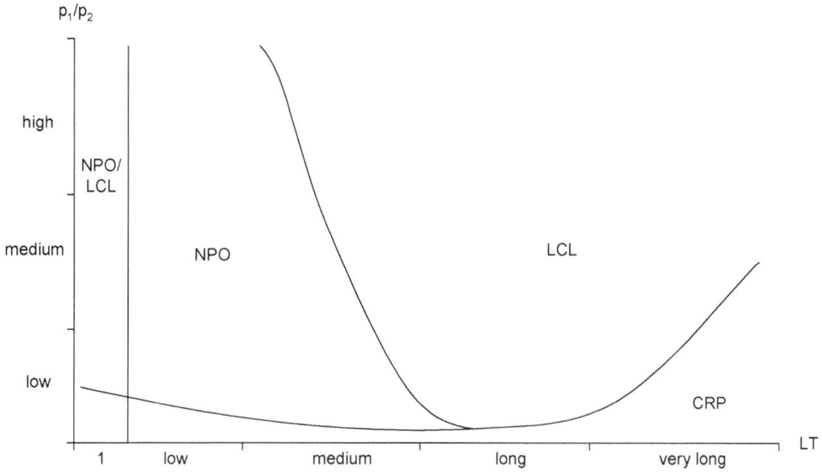

Figure 11.7: When to apply which rationing policy

We applied the suggested dynamic rationing rules to a system with cost-optimal backorder clearing. In such a setting, the constant rationing policy already achieves significant savings over a non-rationing policy. Under other backorder clearing mechanisms, dynamic rationing policies may be far more powerful.

11.5 Proofs

Proof of Proposition 30.

We restrict our attention to the case of $i_t^I > 0$. Otherwise, $cl = 0$ and the claim is trivially true because 0 is the smallest feasible rationing level.

First, we will show that Equation (11.2) is convex in cl: Backorders of class 2 at the end of period t are given by $b_{2t}(cl) = \max\left\{b_{2t-1} + d_{2t} - (i_t^I - cl), 0\right\}$. Taking into account the range of cl we obtain $b_{2t}(cl) = b_{2t-1} + d_{2t} - (i_t^I - cl)$ which is linear and thus convex in cl. Inventory on hand at the end of period t is given by $ih_t(cl) = \max\left\{i_t^I - b_{2t-1} - d_{2t}, cl\right\}$ which equals cl for all feasible cl and is hence convex in cl. Finally,

$$EB_{1t+1}(cl) = E[D_{1t+1} - ih_t - d_{t-LT}]^+ = E[D_{1t+1} - cl - d_{t-LT}]^+.$$

is convex because the maximum operator preserves convexity. Therefore, Equation (11.2) is convex as positive linear combination of convex functions.

By convexity, the minimizer of Equation (11.2) is thus the smallest cl such that

$$\begin{aligned} &p_2\ b_{2t}(cl) + h\ ih_t(cl) + p_1\ EB_{1t+1}(cl) \\ &-p_2\ b_{2t}(cl+1) - h\ ih_t(cl+1) - p_1\ EB_{1t+1}(cl+1) \leq 0 \end{aligned} \tag{11.5}$$

Let $k = i_t^I - b_{2t-1} - d_{2t}$. We may then rewrite the left hand-side of Inequality (11.5) as

$$\begin{aligned} & p_2\ (cl-k) + h\ cl + p_1 \sum_{j=cl+d_{t-LT}} (j - cl - d_{t-LT})\Pr(D_{1t+1} = j) \\ & - p_2\ (cl+1-k) - h\ (cl+1) \\ & -p_1 \sum_{j=cl+1+d_{t-LT}} (j - cl - 1 - d_{t-LT})\Pr(D_{1t+1} = j) \\ = \ & -p_2 - h + p_1 \sum_{j=cl+1+d_{t-LT}} \Pr(D_{1t+1} = j). \end{aligned}$$

With this we obtain

$$\begin{aligned} & -p_2 - h + p_1 \sum_{j=cl+1+d_{t-LT}} \Pr(D_{1t+1} = j) \leq 0 \\ \Leftrightarrow \quad & \sum_{j=cl+1+d_{t-LT}} \Pr(D_{1t+1} = j) \leq \frac{p_2 + h}{p_1} \end{aligned}$$

which completes the proof. □

Proof of Proposition 31.

The sample-path proof of Corollary 2 does not explicitly use the fact that the critical level is the same over all periods. Thus the results carry over to all settings in which one critical or order-up-to level is always higher than the other one. We can then transfer this knowledge to the steady state taking long-term averages.

The dynamic rationing policy allows a critical level of above zero. Thus for any period t the critical level CL_t^{NPC} exceeds CL^{CRP}. Thus the results of Corollary 2 carries over to this case and an increase in the rationing level leads to lower class 1 backorders and higher class 2 backorders and inventory on hand at the end of a period. □

Proof of Proposition 32.

The proof is completely analogous to that of Proposition 31. □

Chapter 12

Conclusion and Critical Review

In this thesis, we have studied a periodic review inventory model with segmented customer. We assumed backordering and a positive (constant) lead time. Applying a new modeling approach, we have optimized a constant critical level policy under average cost criterion for two situations: In the one case, the two customer classes have been prioritized by penalty costs. In the other case, they have been prioritized based on service requirements. We have also looked into dynamic rationing policies.

In this chapter, we conclude this thesis summarizing the main contributions. We will critically review the assumptions of our model and give some indications for future research on inventory rationing.

12.1 Contributions

It was our main objective to provide and solve a mathematical model for situations that differ from existing literature in a couple of ways: Orders are placed at discrete time instances, non-unit-sized demands occur, and demands are not observed one after the other. The model we presented

K. Möllering, *Inventory Rationing*, Edition KWV,
https://doi.org/10.1007/978-3-658-24255-8_12

addresses these issues and contributes to the literature on inventory rationing in several aspects.

As a major contribution, we present and solve the first periodic review model that assumes optimal backorder clearing and this in the presence of a positive lead time. To achieve this contribution, we developed a new modeling approach: We show that class 2 backorders are fundamental for the inventory system, derive their steady state probabilities from an $(LT + 1)$-dimensional Markov chain and follow all other expectation from those. This approach additionally allows us to gain insight into the steady state behavior of all cost drivers, i.e., backorders and inventory level. Studying sample paths, we derive monotonicity properties. The numerical optimization assuming penalty costs as means of prioritization is based on a convexity result and an upper bound for the difference in the policy parameters S (order-up-to level) and CL (critical level).

The second important contribution concerns solving not only the pure cost minimization problem, but also the service-constraint inventory rationing problem. Despite its practical importance - contracts often require a certain degree of service - this problem has attracted very little attention in the literature before. The only other work addressing a critical level policy with service constraints under periodic review (Tempelmeier 2006) applies a non-optimal backorder clearing mechanism and restricts its attention to Poisson demands. Applying the monotonicity results mentioned before, we found that the parameter constellation that just satisfies both α- or β-service level constraints might not always be optimal. Instead, it might be beneficial to satisfy more demands of class 2 customers than originally required. The numerical optimization is now based on a search along the parameter constellations that just fulfill the service requirements of the high priority class while at the same time satisfying the low priority constraints.

As a third contribution, we address the lacking characterization of the optimal (presumably state-dependent) critical level policy under periodic review. We suggest two rules for determining state-dependent rationing levels that both satisfy some intuitive characteristics: If we expect high incoming orders in the near future, the rationing level is lower. We emphasize events in the next period or near future and put lower or no weight on events in the far future. Furthermore, both dynamic rationing policies are still easy to implement. Simulation-based experiments exhibit structural behavior in the savings compared to a constant rationing policy. Our dynamic rationing policies are particularly useful for high differences in penalty costs and longer lead times.

12.2 Critical Review

Research-on-hand contributes to the existing literature on inventory rationing in several ways. Nonetheless, before applying our model to a real setting, our assumptions and requirements should be reviewed carefully. In this section, we will look into the assumptions made and the modeling approach we chose.

Most of our assumptions are in line with existing research on inventory control. However, they may not be found in practice. This concerns for instance the assumption of complete backordering. In most situations, only some of the customers will agree to wait for a delivery and others will leave. Another issue refers to the deterministic and constant lead time. Typically, lead times vary, e.g. due to capacitated supply facilities or exceptional events such as strikes or catastrophes. Unfortunately, these effects cannot be covered with our multi-dimensional Markov chain. This Markov-chain based modeling approach also requires independent, identically distributed demands for each period. Relaxing this assumption, the Markov property will be violated. However, for instance in the case of spare parts, it may well play a role if a significant amount of items has just been replaced, e.g. following a warning of the original manufacturer.

Other aspects that have to be mentioned here relate to the modeling approach. Firstly, the state space increases strongly with the lead time which leads to a memory-intense and time-consuming numerical solution. Also, the model is limited to two customer classes. To extend it to multiple customer classes, it seems more promising to utilize a Markov chain with states $(i_t, b_{1t}, ..., b_{nt}, d_{t-1}, ..., d_{t-LT})$ instead of sticking to an iterative approach, starting with the lowest class of backorders and ending with the inventory on hand at the end of a period. Otherwise, the numerical solution becomes very lengthy and complex, especially concerning the backorder distributions for those customer classes of neither high nor low priority. Deriving structural results would still require our iterative approach.

The last aspect that has given rise to discussion is our backorder clearing mechanism. If backorders were cleared depending on the order of arrival and independent of priority, this would reduce the waiting time for low priority customers. Thus, there is a trade-off between costs and customer service. However, in our numerical experiments the maximum expected amount of class 2 backorders has been well below 1. Thus, although our backorder clearing leads to more class 2 backorders, we hardly observed customers waiting for more than one period.

12.3 Future Research

In Chapter 7.6, we have seen that in particular when it comes to periodic review or continuous review (s, Q)-policies, literature on inventory rationing is lacking exact results. This thesis has addressed some open questions. However, we feel that there is still work to be done. In particular, we see potential in three areas.

The first stream of future research immediately relates to our presented results. We have already indicated a possibility to extend our work to an arbitrary number of customer classes. As far as we can see, such an extension increases the number of dimensions of each state even further. Thus an improved numerical solution would become even more important. In particular, a more efficient algorithm for solving the Markov chain could be applied.

More important from a theoretical point of view are extensions of our work to more general settings. For instance, allowing fixed order cost would add a significant contribution. In this case, it might be possible to apply a similar analysis by limiting to policies with two pairs of parameter constellations: The one pair, (S, CL_1), defines the rationing level and order-up-to level if an order is placed, the other pair, $(0, CL_2)$, applies if no order is placed. Additionally, a parameter s determines the reorder point.

Finally, dynamic rationing under periodic review has not been fully understood. While it seems hard to completely characterize the optimal policy in the presence of lead time *and* backordering, the key factors driving dynamic rationing levels should be better understood. Our simulation study underlined the intuition that a dynamic rationing rule should put more emphasis on the near future than on the far future. Another factor that could directly influence a state-dependent critical level are the existing backorders of the low priority customers. High amounts of class 2 backorders could lead to a lower rationing level because the cost associated with them might be worth the higher risk of future class 1 backorders. The rationing level CL and the order-up-to level S can be seen as controls in the sense of stochastic dynamic control theory. Then, numerical studies, e.g. employing the Howard algorithm, also referred to as policy iteration (Howard 1960), could shed additional insight into the optimal controls.

Eventually, we sum up that for situations with a segmented customer basis inventory rationing and in particular the critical level policy provide a means to increase profits substantially. However, for a lot of practical situations, e.g. with additional setup cost, characterizing the optimal policy remains an open task.

Bibliography

Abramowitz, M. (1950). *Inventories and Business Cycles.* New York: National Bureau of Economic Research.

Arrow, K., T. Harris, and J. Marschak (1951). Optimal Inventory Policy. *Econometrica 19*, 250–272.

Arslan, H., S. Graves, and T. Roemer (2005). A Single-Product Inventory Model for Multiple Demand Classes. Working paper, Suffolk University and MIT, USA.

Ash, R. and R. Bischop (1972). Monopoly as a Markov Process. *Mathematics Magazine 45*, 26–29.

Äxsater, S. (2000). *Inventory Control.* Amsterdam: Kluwer.

Äxsater, S., M. Kleijn, and T. D. Kok (2004). Stock rationing in a continuous review two-echelon inventory model. *Annals of Operations Research 126*, 177–194.

Bagchi, U., J. Hayya, and C. Chu (1986). The Effect of Lead-Time Variability: The Case of Independent Demand. *Journal of Operations Management 6*, 159–177.

Barge, W. (2002). *Autonomous Solution Methods for Large-Scale Markov Chains.* Ph. D. thesis, Department of Operations Research, University of North Carolina, USA.

Belobaba, P. (1989). Application of a Probabilistic Decision Model to Airline Seat Inventory Control. *Operations Research 37*, 183–197.

K. Möllering, *Inventory Rationing*, Edition KWV,
https://doi.org/10.1007/978-3-658-24255-8

Blinder, A. and L. Maccini (1991). Taking Stock: A Critical Assessment of Recent Research on Inventories. *Journal of Economic Perspectives 5*, 73–96.

Bonini, C., W. Hausman, and H. Bierman (1997). *Quantitative Analysis for Management* (9th ed.). Boston et al.: McGraw-Hill / Irwin.

Borovkov, K. (2003). *Elements of Stochastic Modeling.* Singapore: World Scientific Publishing.

Bozarth, C. and R. Handfield (2005). *Introduction to Operations and Supply Chain Management.* Boston et al.: McGraw-Hill.

Brown, R. (1967). *Decision Rules for Inventory Management.* Hinsdale: Dryden Press.

Bylina, B. and J. Bylina (2004). A review of numerical methods for solving large Markov chains. In *First EuroNGI Workshop: New Trends in Modelling, Quantitative Methods and Measurements.*

Cachon, G. and C. Terwiesch (2006). *Matching Supply with Demand.* Boston et al.: McGraw-Hill.

Callioni, G., X. de Montgros, R. Slagmulder, L. van Wassenhove, and L. Wright (2005, March). Inventory-Driven Costs. *Harvard Business Review.*

Chen, H., M. Frank, and O. Wu (2005). The inventories of American companies between 1981 and 2000. *Management Science 51*, 1015–1031.

Cohen, M., P. Kleindorfer, and H. Lee (1998). Service Constrained (s,S) Inventory Systems with Priority Demand Classes and Lost Sales. *Management Science 34*, 482–499.

de Véricourt, F., F. Karaesman, and Y. Dallery (2002). Optimal Stock Allocation for a Capacitated Supply System. *Management Science 48*, 1486–1501.

de Véricourt, F., F. Karaesmen, and Y. Dallery (2001). Assessing the Benefits of Different Stock Allocation Policies for a Make-to-Stock Production System. *Manufacturing and Service Operations Management 3*, 105–121.

Dekker, R., R. Hill, M. Kleijn, and R. Teunter (2002). On the (S-1,S) Lost Sales Inventory Model with Priority Demand Classes. *Naval Research Logistics 49*, 593–610.

Dekker, R., M. Kleijn, and P. de Rooij (1998). A Spare Parts Stocking Policy Based on Equipment Criticality. *International Journal of Production Economics 56-57*, 69–77.

Deshpande, V., M. Cohen, and K. Donohue (2003). A Threshold Inventory Rationing Policy for Service-Differentiated Demand Classes. *Management Science 49*, 683–703.

Dümbgen, L. (2003). *Stochastik für Informatiker.* New York: Springer.

Edgeworth, F. (1888). The Mathematical Theory of Banking. *Journal of the Royal Statistical Society 5*, 13–27.

Enders, P., I. Adan, and G. van Houtum (2006). A Mixed Lost-Sales Backordering Inventory Problem with two Customer Classes. Working paper, Carnegie Mellon University, USA, and Technische Universiteit Eindhoven, Netherlands.

Eppen, G. and L. Schrage (1981). Centralized Ordering Policies in a Multi-Warehouse System with Lead Time and Random Demand. In L. Schwarz (Ed.), *Multi-Level Production/Inventory Control Systems: Theory and Practice.* Amsterdam: North-Holland.

Evans, R. (1968). Sales and restocking policies in a single item inventory system. *Management Science 14*, 463–472.

Fadiloglu, M. and Ö. Bulut (2005). An Embedded Markov Chain Approach to the Analysis of Inventory Systems with Backordering Under Rationing. Working paper, Bilkent University, Turkey.

Fitzsimmons, J. and M. Fitzsimmons (2005). *Service Management.* Boston et al.: McGraw-Hill.

Frank, K., R. Zhang, and I. Duenyas (2003). Optimal Policies for Inventory Systems with Priority Demand Classes. *Operations Research 51*, 993–1002.

Freedman, D. (1983). *Approximating Countable Markov Chains* (2nd ed.). New York: Springer.

Gayon, J.-P., S. Benjaafar, and F. de Véricourt (2004). Using Imperfect Demand Information in Production-Inventory Systems with Multiple Customer Classes. Working paper, Ecole Central Paris, France, and University of Minnesota, USA, and Duke University, USA.

Gayon, J.-P., F. de Véricourt, F. Karaesman, and Y. Dallery (2005). Stock Rationing in a Multi-Class Make-To-Stock Queue with Information on the Production Status. Working paper, Ecole Central Paris, France, and Duke University, USA, and Koc University, Turkey.

Gibson, D. and E. Seneta (1987). Augmented Truncations of Infinite Stochastic Matrices. *Journal of Applied Probability 24*, 600–608.

Grassmann, W. (1993). Rounding Errors in Certain Algorithms Involving Markov Chains. *ACM transactions on Mathematical Software 19*, 496–508.

Grassmann, W., M. Taksar, and D. Heyman (1985). Regeneratice Analysis and Steady State Distributions for Markov Chains. *Operations Research 33*, 1107–1116.

Ha, A. (1997a). Inventory Rationing in a Make-to-Stock Production System with Several Demand Classes and Lost Sales. *Management Science 43*, 1093–1103.

Ha, A. (1997b). Inventory Rationing in a Make-to-Stock Production System with Two Priority Classes and Backordering. *Naval Research Logistics 44*, 458–472.

Ha, A. (2000). Stock Rationing in a M/Ek/1 Make-to-Stock Queue. *Management Science 46*, 77–87.

Hammond, J. (1994). Barilla SpA. Case Study 9-694-046, Harvard Business School.

Harris, F. (1913). How Many Parts to Make at Once. *Factory, The Magazine of Management 10*, 135–36.

Hayes, R. and D. Garvin (1982). Managing as if tomorrow mattered. *Harvard Business Review 60*, 70–79.

Howard, R. (1960). *Dynamic Programming and Markov Processes.* New York: John Wiley and Sons.

Iglehart, D. (1963). Optimality of (s,S) Policies in the Infinite Horizon Dynamic Inventory Problem. *Management Science 9*, 259–267.

Isaacson, D. and R. Madsen (1976). *Markov Chains - Theory and Applications.* New York: John Wiley and Sons.

Jackson, P. (1988). Stock allocation in a two-echelon distribution system or "what to do until your ship comes in". *Management Science 34*, 880–895.

Kamae, T., U. Krengel, and G. O'Brien (1997). Stochastic inequalities on partially ordered spaces. *Annals of Probability 5*, 899–912.

Kaplan, A. (1968). Stock Rationing. *Management Science 15*, 260–267.

Katircioglu, K. and D. Atkins (1998). Managing Inventory for Multiple Customer Classes Requiring Different Levels of Service. Working paper, IBM T.J.Watson Research Center, USA, and University of British Columbia, Canada.

Khouja, M. (1999). The single-period (news-vendor) problem: litature review and suggestions for future research. *Omega 27*, 537–553.

Kleijn, M. and R. Dekker (1998). An Overview of Inventory Systems with Several Demand Classes. Econometric Institute Report 9838/A, Rotterdam, Netherlands.

Kranenburg, A. and G. van Houtum (2006a). Cost Optimization in the (S-1,S) Lost Sales Inventory Model with Multiple Demand Classes. Working paper, Technische Universiteit Eindhoven, Netherlands.

Kranenburg, A. and G. van Houtum (2006b). Service Differentiation in Spare Parts Inventory Management. Working paper, Technische Universiteit Eindhoven, Netherlands.

Krengel, U. (2002). *Einführung in die Wahrscheinlichkeitstheorie und Statistik* (6th ed.). Braunschweig: Vieweg.

Lal, R. and U. Bhat (1988). Reduced System Algorithms for Markov Chains. *Management Science 34*, 1202–1220.

Lambert, D., J. Stock, and L. Ellram (1998). *Fundamentals of Logistics Management*. Boston et al.: McGraw-Hill / Irwin.

Leenders, M. (2005). *Purchasing and Supply Chain Management*. Boston et al.: McGraw-Hill.

Li, H. and Y. Zhao (2000). Stochastic Block-Monotonicity in the Approximation of the stationary distribution of Infinite Markov Chains. *Stochastic Models 16*, 313–333.

Lindvall, T. (2002). *Lectures on the Coupling Method*. Mineola: Dover Publications.

Magee, J. (1958). *Production Planning and Inventory Control*. New York: McGraw-Hill.

McGill, J. and G. van Ryzin (1999). Revenue Management: Research Overview and Prospects. *Transportation Science 33*, 233–256.

Melchiors, P. (2003). Restricted Time-Remebering Policies for the Inventory Rationing Problem. *International Journal of Production Economics 81-82*, 461–468.

Melchiors, P., R. Dekker, and M. Kleijn (2000). Inventory Rationing in an (s,Q) Inventory Model with Lost Sales and Two Demand Classes. *Journal of the Operational Research Society 51*, 111–122.

Merlo, A., B. Sericola, and R. Marie (1996). A new Stable Algorithm for Computing Steady State Measures for Markov Chains. IRISA Publication Interne 1038, Rennes, France.

Moon, I. and S. Kang (1998). Rationing Policies for Some Inventory Systems. *Journal of the Operational Research Society 49*, 509–518.

Nahmias, S. (2005). *Production and Operations Analysis* (5th ed.). Boston et al.: McGraw-Hill.

Nahmias, S. and W. Demmy (1981). Operating Characteristics of an Inventory System with Rationing. *Management Science 27*, 1236–1245.

Neuts, M. (1995). *Matrix-Geometric Solutions in Stochastic Models: An Algorithmic Approach.* Mineola: Dover Publications.

Page, L., S. Brin, R. Motwani, and T. Winograd (1998). The PageRank Citation Ranking: Bringing Order to the Web. *Stanford Digital Libraries.*

Philippe, B., Y. Saad, and W. Stewart (1992). Numerical Methods in Markov Chain Modelling. *Operations Research 40*, 1156–1179.

Porteus, E. (2002). *Foundations of Stochastic Inventory Theory.* Stanford: Stanford University Press.

Rabiner, L. (1989). A Tutorial on Hidden Markov Chains and Selected Applications in Speech Recognition. *Proceedings of the IEEE 77*, 257–286.

Ross, S. (1983). *Stochastic Processes.* New York: John Wiley and Sons.

Scarf, H. (1959). The Optimality of (S,s) policies in the Dynamic Inventory Problem. In K. Arrow, S. Karlin, and H. Scarf (Eds.), *Mathematical Methods in the Social Sciences*, pp. 196–202. Stanford: Stanford University Press.

Schneider, H. (1979). The Service Level in Inventory Control Systems. *Engineering and Process Economics 4*, 341–348.

Schneider, H. (1981). Effect of Service-Levels on Order-Points and Order-Levels in Inventory Models. *International Journal of Production Research 19*, 615–631.

Seneta, E. (2006). *Non-negative Matrices and Markov Chains* (2nd ed.). New York: Springer.

Sheskin, T. (1985). A Markov Chain Partitioning Algorithm for Computing Steady State Probabilities. *Operations Research 33*, 228–235.

Shiryaev, A. (1996). *Probability* (2nd ed.). New York: Springer.

Shugan, S. and S. Radas (2006). Services and Seasonal Demand. Working paper, University of Florida and Washington University, USA.

Silver, E., D. Pyke, and R. Peterson (1998). *Inventory Management and Production Planning and Scheduling.* New York: JohnWiley and Sons.

Song, J. (1994). The Effect of Leadtime Uncertainty in a Simple Stochastic Inventory Model. *Management Science 40*, 603–613.

Stewart, W. (1994). *Introduction to the Numerical Solution of Markov Chains.* Princeton: Princeton University Press.

Stoyan, D. (1983). *Comparison methods for queues and other stochastic models.* New York: John Wiley and Sons.

Swaminathan, J. and H. Lee (2003). Design for postponement. In A. de Kok and S. Graves (Eds.), *Supply Chain Management: Design, Coordination and Operation*, Chapter 5, pp. 199–226. Amsterdam: Elsevier.

Tempelmeier, H. (2006). Supply Chain Inventory Optimization with Two Customer Classes in Discrete Time. *to appear in: European Journal of Operational Research.*

Thonemann, U. (2005). *Operations Management.* Munich: Pearson Studium.

Tijms, H. (1994). *Stochastic Models - An Algorithmic Approach.* New York: John Wiley and Sons.

Tijms, H. and M. van de Coevering (1991). A simple Numerical Approach for Infinite-State Markov Chains. *Probability in the Engineering and Informational Sciences 5*, 285–295.

Topkis, D. (1968). Optimal Ordering and Rationing Policies in a Nonstationary Dynamic Inventory Model. *Management Science 15*, 160–176.

Tsay, A., S. Nahmias, and N. Agrawal (1999). Modeling Supply Chain Contracts: A Review. In S. Tayur, R. Ganeshan, and M. Magazine (Eds.), *Quantitative Models for Supply Chain Management*, Chapter 10, pp. 299–336. Norwell: Kluwer.

Tweedie, R. (1998). Truncation approximations of invariant measures for Markov Chains. *Journal of Applied Probability 35*, 517–536.

van Ryzin, G. and K. Talluri (2005). An Introduction to Revenue Management. In H. Green and J. Smith (Eds.), *Tutorials in Operations Reseach*, Chapter 6, pp. 142–192. INFORMS.

Veinott, A. (1965a). Optimal policy for a multi-product, dynamic, nonstationary inventory problem. *Management Science 12*, 206–222.

Veinott, A. (1965b). Optimal Policy in a Dynamic, Non-Stationary Inventory Model with Several Demand Classes. *Operations Research 13*, 761–778.

Walther, G. (1996). *Upside-Down Marketing: Turning Your Ex-Customers into Your Best Customers* (reissue ed.). Boston et al.: McGraw-Hill.

White, D. (1985). Real Applications of Markov Decision Processes. *Interfaces 15*, 73–83.

White, D. (1988). Further Real Applications of Markov Decision Processes. *Interfaces 18*, 55–61.

Whitin, T. (1957). *Theory of Inventory Management.* Princeton: Princeton University Press.

Wolff, R. (1989). *Stochastic Modeling and the Theory of Queues.* Upper Saddle River: Prentice Hall.

Yano, C. and H. Lee (1995). Lot Sizing with Random Yields. *Operations Research 43*, 311–334.

Zhao, Y., W. Braun, and W. Li (1999). Northwest Corner and Banded Matrix Approximations to a Countable Markov Chain. *Naval Research Logistics 46*, 187–197.

Zhao, Y. and D. Liu (1996). The Censored Markov Chain and the Best Augmentation. *Journal of Applied Probability 33*, 623–629.

Zheng, Z. (2005). *Learning Probability Models and Quantitative Finance.* University of Wisconsin-Milwaukee, USA. Available at: www.wuwm.edu/ ziyu/mc.pdf.

Zipkin, P. (2000). *Foundations of Inventory Management.* Boston et al.: McGraw-Hill.

MIX
Papier aus verantwortungsvollen Quellen
Paper from responsible sources
FSC® C105338

If you have any concerns about our products,
you can contact us on
ProductSafety@springernature.com

In case Publisher is established outside the EU,
the EU authorized representative is:
Springer Nature Customer Service Center GmbH
Europaplatz 3, 69115 Heidelberg, Germany

Printed by Libri Plureos GmbH
in Hamburg, Germany